A London Peculiar

A London Peculiar

THE LONDON YOU SHOULDN'T MISS

RAFE HEYDEL-MANKOO

First published in 2015 by New Holland Publishers Pty Ltd
London • Sydney • Auckland

The Chandlery Unit 009 50 Westminster Bridge Road
London SE1 7QY United Kingdom
$1/66$ Gibbes Street Chatswood NSW 2067 Australia
218 Lake Road Northcote Auckland New Zealand

www.newhollandpublishers.com

A record of this book is held at the British Library and the
National Library of Australia.

ISBN 9781742575735

Managing Director: Fiona Schultz
Publisher: Alan Whiticker
Editor: Holly Willsher
Designer: Andrew Davies
Production Director: Olga Dementiev
Printer: Toppan Leefung Printing Ltd

10 9 8 7 6 5 4 3 2 1

Keep up with New Holland Publishers on Facebook
www.facebook.com/NewHollandPublishers

CONTENTS

DEDICATION

To my mother and father

ACKNOWLEDGEMENTS

I am grateful to Alan Whiticker and New Holland Publishers for their commitment to this project and for their patience as the manuscript reached completion. I would like to thank the many institutions who have graciously supplied photographs for inclusion in this book and Dirk Seyfried at James J. Fox for the patience with which he handled my requests. I am indebted to Rupert Meacher for the loan of his photographic equipment, without which this book may not have been possible. I am also grateful to Hugh Macpherson for his numerous kindnesses and to Peter Whittle, a fellow Londoner, for his enthusiasm and encouragement. Thanks are also due to Giovanni Zappulo, Pawel Ben Gheshir and Robert Knight. Finally, I would like to thank my parents, for everything.

Next page spread: Gentrified houses on Fournier Street, Spitalfields.

Following page: The 15th century open undercroft beneath Lincoln's Inn Chapel. Up until the 19th century, young mothers often left their babies here to be adopted by the Inn, with many such children subsequently named "Lincoln".

INTRODUCTION

"London goes beyond any boundary or convention. It contains every wish or word ever spoken, every action or gesture ever made, every harsh or noble statement ever expressed. It is illimitable. It is Infinite London."

PETER ACKROYD. *London: The Biography*

For an author, the greatest challenge in writing a book about London is not what to put in but what to leave out. Two thousand years old, its densely packed population equal to that of Scotland and Wales combined, London is a city bursting with historical bounty and filled with the fruits of human endeavour. It is a city state in all but name – and a lifetime spent in earnest exploration of its vast expanse will not yield every secret.

A London Peculiar is an insider's guide to some of the most unusual, unique and intriguing hidden gems to be found in the city. Countless books have been published about London's grand and celebrated attractions and a small number examine the less familiar – but *A London Peculiar* delves deeper into the fertile field of London esoterica, revealing a remarkable array of little-known curiosities, many of which are published here for the first time.

The extremely diverse range of entries included within these pages makes this book itself something of a curiosity. Whether a museum, a pub or a lamppost, all of the carefully selected subjects are given equal treatment – story trumps size. Famous landmarks and attractions are not featured except in passing: and so a section on Trafalgar Square ignores the National Gallery while St. Paul's Cathedral is only mentioned in connection with two obscure inscriptions.

Structured by subject rather than by area or borough, *A London Peculiar* is intended to be more than a guide book about hidden London. By grouping shops, houses, pubs, museums and other attractions into separate chapters, it is hoped that the reader will develop a greater feel for the diverse character of London, as well as an appreciation for the richness of its heritage. London is a city in which every step taken passes through the shadows of those who came before and this theme is explored in subsections that trace the city of Charles Dickens and Ian Fleming's James Bond.

A London Peculiar is unapologetically nostalgic. The author has a passion for the history, traditions and institutions of London and believes that much of the city's charm is contained in its secret corners. This book is a means of conveying some of that knowledge so that others can share in the same delights and discover the hidden treasures that lie just below the surface – for even the dullest street contains magic for those who know where to look.

RAFE HEYDEL-MANKOO

CHAPTER ONE

MUSEUMS

Paris may have more cinemas and New York more theatres, but London is the undisputed museum capital of the world. No city can compete with the city's mind-boggling collection of more than 240 museums, three of which are amongst the world's ten most visited and six of which are amongst the top twenty.

The British Museum, the world's oldest national public museum, is part of a unique category of world-class institutions and continues to stand its ground with its two great heavyweight rivals: the Louvre in Paris and the Metropolitan Museum of Art in New York. At the other end of the spectrum, scattered across the length and breadth of London, are a staggering selection of small, specialised museums devoted to the fascinating, the esoteric and the arcane. Fortunately, it is not necessary to be a scholar or collector of recondite information to appreciate these intimate institutions. The curators of most museum collections are keen to attract a wide audience and the displays invariably engage and entertain. And so, after only a week in London, visitors may find themselves unexpected experts in the history of subjects as diverse as fans, tea, motorcycles, steam engines, crime and medicine.

Left: Specimen jars at the Grant Museum of Zoology and Comparative Anatomy

The Alexander Fleming Laboratory Museum

Few discoveries have benefitted humanity more than Professor Alexander Fleming's discovery of penicillin in his cramped laboratory at St. Mary's Hospital in 1928. Before penicillin, doctors had no means of treating infections such as pneumonia or rheumatic fever, and a small cut or scratch from a rose bush or rusty nail could easily result in blood poisoning and death. Fleming's Nobel Prize-winning discovery heralded the age of antibiotics and continues to save countless millions of lives.

The Museum has restored Fleming's laboratory to its 1928 condition and it is a popular filming location. Through displays and videos visitors can explore the fascinating history of Fleming's discovery and the later development of penicillin. In 1999 the laboratory was declared an International Historic Chemical Landmark by the Royal Society of Chemistry and the American Chemical Society.

The Alexander Fleming Laboratory Museum, St. Mary's Hospital, Praed Street, London, W2 1NY

W: www.imperial.nhs.uk/aboutus/ourorganisation/museumsandarchives/index.htm
T: +44 (0)20 3312 6528
OPEN: Mon–Thu 10am–1pm
U: Paddington
ADMISSION: Free

Visitors can arrange to visit at other times by prior arrangement.

KEY
U: = nearest Underground station
ADMISSION: £ = fees apply

Right: The Alexander Fleming Laboratory Museum

The Cinema Museum

The Cinema Museum (London) is home to an eclectic treasure trove of artefacts gathered by two passionate cinema-going enthusiasts: Ronald Grant and Martin Humphries. In 1986, realising that their personal collections were of national significance, the two enthusiasts decided to join forces and found the Cinema Museum. Since 1998 the museum has been housed in Kennington's imposing Lambeth Workhouse, a noteworthy building for cinema buffs as it was here that the young Charlie Chaplin and his destitute mother once lived.

The Cinema Museum is delightfully idiosyncratic and unapologetically nostalgic. This is a museum for lovers of film production, cinema paraphernalia and the experience of cinema-going as much as the films themselves. Ushers' uniforms, popcorn cartons, projectors, seats, posters and ashtrays recall the evolution of cinemas, from the silent era through to today. British cinema has never possessed the glamour of Hollywood and, perhaps appropriately, this is not the place for those seeking a slick, state-of-the-art museum filled with hi-tech interactive displays about box office blockbusters.

The heart of the collection remains the huge number of artefacts saved from the destruction of the James F. Donald cinemas of Aberdeen, the city in which Ronald Grant started work as an apprentice projectionist at the age of 15. The museum runs a wide range of events, talks and screenings, often staffed by dedicated volunteers dressed in cinema employees' period costumes.

The Cinema Museum, 2 Dugard Way (off Renfrew Road), London, SE11 4TH
w: www.cinemamuseum.org.uk
t: +44 (0)20 7840 2200
u: Elephant & Castle
ADMISSION: £

Guided tours of the museum are available most days but it is essential that these are booked in advance so that volunteer guides can be arranged. The museum is not otherwise open to the public.

Above: The Cinema Museum is housed in the Lambeth Workhouse, once the home of Charlie Chaplin

Below: Exhibits at The Cinema Museum

The Foundling Museum

The Foundling Museum in Brunswick Square recounts the history of the Foundling Hospital, a children's home established in 1739 by the philanthropist Captain Thomas Coram for the "education and maintenance of exposed and deserted young children". The 18th century was an era of enlightened social campaigning and moral philanthropy; and the tragedy and disgrace of the 1,000 children and babies abandoned each year (usually due to illegitimacy or poverty), spurred Coram to establish this hospital as the nation's first children's charity. Amongst the museum's saddest artefacts are the "foundling tokens", everyday items such as buttons or coins pinned by mothers to their children as a means of identification in the vain hope that they might one day seek their return.

Above: The Foundling Museum in Brunswick Square

Left: The Court Room at The Foundling Museum

The Hospital was a terrific success in fashionable Georgian society. The artist William Hogarth, a founding governor of the Hospital actively involved in its early history, seized on the institution's popularity as a means to promote British art. Hogarth initiated the hospital's collection in 1740 by donating a magnificent portrait of Thomas Coram that he had painted to commemorate the signing of the hospital's founding charter by George II. Encouraged by Hogarth, a number of the era's other great artists also donated artworks in support of the hospital, thus creating the nation's first public gallery.

The paintings of Thomas Gainsborough, Allan Ramsay, Joshua Reynolds, Louis-Francois Roubiliac and John Michael Rysbrack transformed the hospital into a forerunner of the Royal Academy.

Today the Foundling Hospital Art Collection is of national significance and whilst its greatest treasures are from the 18th and 19th centuries, it continues to expand. In 2010 the Museum acquired the bronze cast *Baby Things, Mitten*, by Britart superstar Tracey Emin. This tiny cast of a baby's mitten is inspired by the foundling tokens and is permanently displayed on a railing outside the Museum, behind the statue of Thomas Coram.

In addition to the foundlings, Thomas Coram and William Hogarth, The Foundling Museum also tells the story of the composer George Frideric Handel, another governor of the hospital and a generous benefactor. Handel's association with the hospital commenced in 1749 when he offered his first benefit concert to help fund the completion of the Chapel, composing the Foundling Hospital Anthem ("Blessed are they that considereth the poor") for the occasion. The concert proved such a success that Handel performed *Messiah* at the Hospital every year until his death in 1759. In his will Handel bequeathed the score of Messiah to the Hospital, and because of this impeccable connection the Foundling Museum is now home to the Gerald Coke Handel Collection, the world's largest private collection of Handel memorabilia.

The Museum, its collections and preserved historic interiors are housed in a refurbished building close to the original location of the Hospital, now a large urban space for children (Coram's Fields).

There is a programme of regular public events including lunchtime concerts, lectures, performances, workshops and family-friendly activities.

The Foundling Museum, 40 Brunswick Square, London, WC1N 1AZ

w: www.foundlingmuseum.org.uk
T: +44 (0)20 7841 3600
OPEN: Mon closed; Tue–Sat 10am–5pm; Sun 11am–5pm
U: Russell Square
ADMISSION: £

The Grant Museum of Zoology and Comparative Anatomy

The Grant Museum of Zoology and Comparative Anatomy is a picture-book example of a museum built upon a 19th century personal collection. Rows of wooden display cabinets filled with carefully posed skeletons and spirit-preserved animals line both floors of the two-storey room. Although it moved to a new location with modern facilities in 2011, the atmosphere of this small museum manages to replicate the feeling of a giant Victorian curio cabinet. Not even state of the art computer display panels detract from the effect, which has been tastefully and imaginatively crafted by the curator and designers. From a jar of moles to a pig foetus and bisected heads, the weird and peculiar items on display can fascinate, bewilder and repulse. Rare specimens in the collection include extinct species such as the dodo and the marsupial wolf. There is also a touch of humour: on the first floor, four humanoid skeletons stand as if peering over the balcony, awaiting your arrival.

The Grant Museum is part of University College London and is the only teaching zoological museum in the city. It was founded in 1828 by Professor Robert Grant (1793–1874), a mentor to Charles Darwin and England's first Professor of Zoology and Comparative Anatomy.

Below: Specimens at The Grant Museum of Zoology

Above: Four skeletons look down on the main floor of the Grant Museum of Zoology

Upon arriving at the University of London to take up the position as Chair, Grant realised that the institution had no teaching materials with which he could instruct his students; he immediately set about building up a collection of specimens, materials and notes. This collection, which Grant bequeathed to the University upon his death, forms the basis of the current museum.

Over the decades, successive chairs and curators have steadily added to the collection. The museum has also inherited or absorbed collections from a number of universities which have closed down their own zoological repositories. Despite some rocky periods, including the destruction of many specimens following a collapsed roof in the 1880s and threatened closure due to funding issues in the 20th century, the museum is now in robust health and has a secure future.

The Grant Museum of Zoology and Comparative Anatomy, Rockefeller Building, University College London, 21 University Street, London, WC1E 6DE
w: www.ucl.ac.uk/museums/zoology
T: +44 (0)20 3108 2052
OPEN: Sun closed; Mon–Sat 1pm–5pm
U: Warren Street; Euston Square
ADMISSION: Free

The Hunterian Museum at the Royal College of Surgeons

London is home to more than twenty museums dedicated to health and medicine – taken together, they could easily fill a two-week holiday and would give new meaning to the phrase "medical tourism". From the Anaesthesia Heritage Centre to the British Dental Association Museum, the range of specialist museums reflects London's well-established position as a centre of medical research and innovation.

The Hunterian Museum at the Royal College of Surgeons is one of the oldest of these institutions, and its esoteric collection of anatomical, pathological and zoological specimens is

Below: The Hunterian Museum at the Royal College of Surgeons

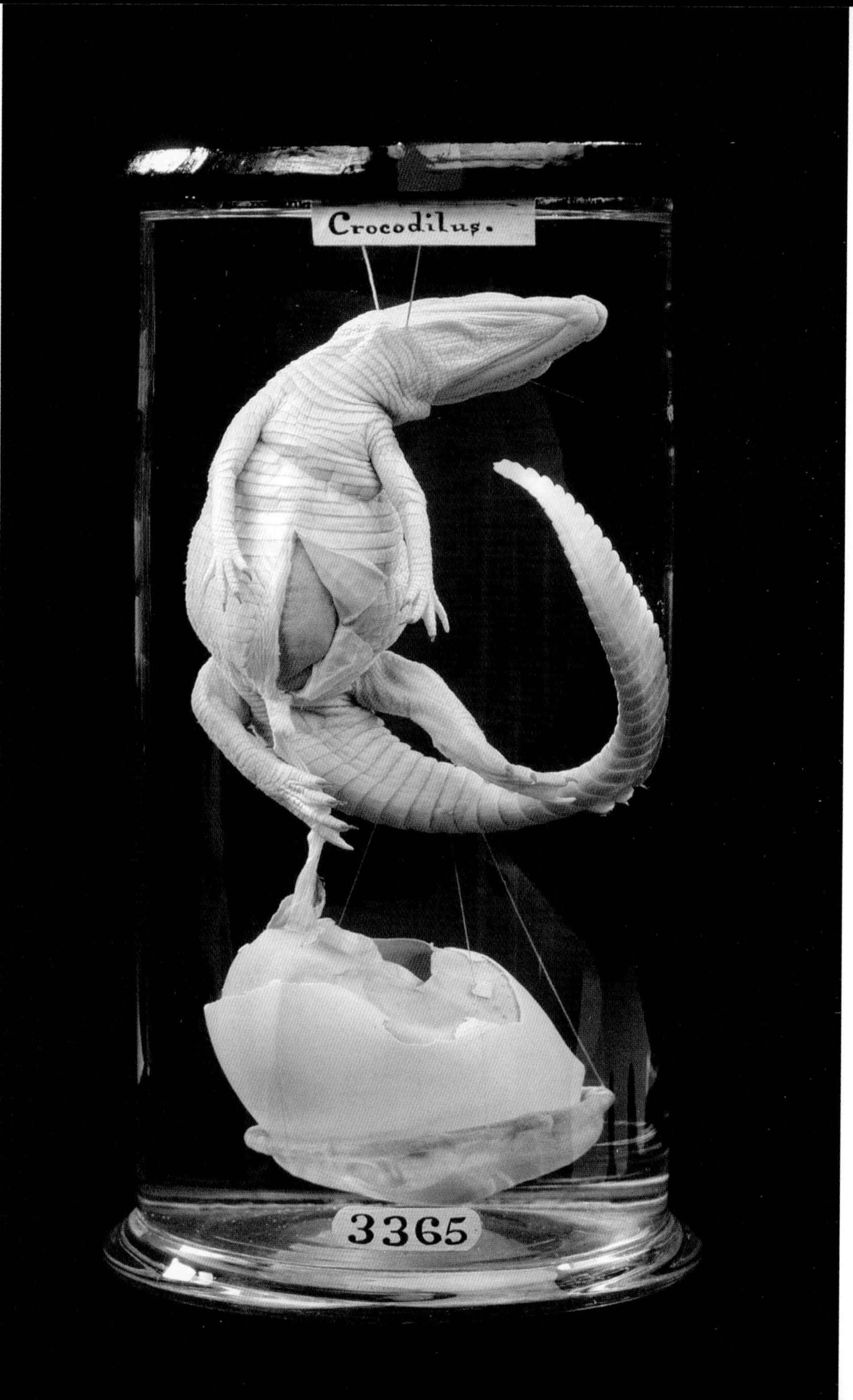
Crocodilus.
3365

one of the most bizarre sights in London. With no need for any of the special effects associated with some deliberately gory tourist attractions, the Hunterian Museum's shock factor exists in the startling authenticity of its artefacts.

Magnificently displayed in impressive glass cabinets is a selection of items from the Hunterian's collection of 6,000 exhibits, including human organs, contorted skeletons, brains eroded by venereal disease, a crocodile foetus with umbilical cord attached to its egg and, perhaps most disturbing, half of a perfectly preserved child's face.

The Museum was born out of the collection from John Hunter (1728–1793), one of the leading surgeons and scientific researchers of his era. Over the course of his career Hunter amassed a personal collection of approximately 15,000 specimens relating to human and animal anatomy. These specimens were housed at his substantial home in Earl's Court, along with a living menagerie that included zebras, buffaloes, mountain goats and jackals. Hunter and his personal zoo are believed to have inspired the fictional character Dr. Doolittle, the Victorian naturalist who could "speak to the animals".

In 1799 the British Government purchased Hunter's collection and presented it to the Company (later The Royal College) of Surgeons. The collection formed the basis for the Hunterian Museum, which was established at the Royal College of Surgeon's new headquarters in Lincoln's Inn Fields, in a building designed by the leading architect George Dance, with later alterations and extensions by Charles Barry, architect of the Houses of Parliament. 10 May 1941 was a sad day for Barry enthusiasts as the Houses of Parliament and the Royal College of Surgeons both suffered direct hits by bombs during the London Blitz. Much of the collection of the Hunterian Museum was lost in this calamity.

The Hunterian Museum constructed after the war was smaller than before but retained some pre-war design features, along with approximately 3,500 of Hunter's original artefacts and another 2,500 acquired after 1799. Between 2003 and 2005 the Hunterian Museum underwent a major programme of refurbishment which also saw it merge with the Odontological Museum (which had been housed in the same building) and the Historical Surgical Instrument Collection. Notable artefacts in the combined collections include the dentures of Winston Churchill, a necklace of human teeth brought back from the Congo by the explorer Henry Stanley, the skeleton of "The Irish Giant" Charles Byrne (1761–1783), and a prosthetic silver nose attached to a pair of glasses in the style of a Groucho Marx fancy-dress kit. The nose was worn by a 19th century woman whose own nose had been destroyed by syphilis.

The Hunterian Museum at the Royal College of Surgeons of England,
35–43 Lincoln's Inn Fields, London, WC2A 3PE

W: www.rcseng.ac.uk/museums/hunterian
T: +44 (0)20 7869 6560
OPEN: Sun–Mon closed; Tue–Sat 10am–5pm
U: Holborn; Temple
ADMISSION: Free

Left: A Crocodile foetus with umbilical cord attached to its egg in The Hunterian Museum at The Royal College of Surgeons.

The Library and Museum of Freemasonry

Freemasonry is renowned for secrecy and mysterious rituals but in recent years its practitioners have attempted to shed light on the history and modern role of "the craft". The Library and Museum of Freemasonry housed in Covent Garden's vast and imposing Freemason's Hall charts the history of English Freemasonry and is home to one of the world's greatest collections of masonic material. Visitors to the museum will not learn strange handshakes – and the secrets of initiation remain closely-guarded secrets – but masonic symbolism and the bewilderingly complex systems of masonic degrees, offices and branches are carefully explained, as are masonic dining habits and charitable causes.

The permanent and temporary exhibits from Masonic lodges around the globe provide a fascinating insight into the evolution of this worldwide fraternal organisation. Notable artefacts include items from famous Freemasons such as Winston Churchill and King Edward VII, and an immense ornate throne commissioned in 1790 by the United Grand Lodge of England for their Grand Master, the Prince of Wales, later King George IV. Amongst the most striking objects are masonic "jewel" badges manufactured from scraps of material (including bone and hair) by Napoleonic French prisoners of war incarcerated in English prisons.

The Museum's large exhibition space also displays many items relating to other fraternal societies, including the Sons of the Phoenix and the Oddfellows.

Freemason's Hall, the richly-decorated centre of English freemasonry, is a

Left: Hand-coloured French Masonic apron, c. 1805. The two pillars depict Joseph Bonaparte and Cambacères, two leading freemasons of the era.

Above: The Temple Doors of Freemason's Hall

magnificent Grade II* listed heritage building which serves as the headquarters for the United Grand Lodge of England, the world's oldest lodge. When the Hall's sumptuous Grand Temple is not in use, The Museum of Freemasonry organises up to five free tours of the building each weekday on a first-come-first-served basis. Saturday tours must be booked in advance.

The Library and Museum of Freemasonry, Freemason's Hall, 60 Great Queen Street, London, WC2B 5AZ

w: www.freemasonry.london.museum

T: +44 (0)20 7395 9257

OPEN: Mon–Fri 10am–5pm

U: Covent Garden

ADMISSION: Free

The Magic Circle Museum

The Magic Circle has been the world's premier society for practicing magicians for more than a century, and over that time it has achieved a reputation for secrecy worthy of *The Da Vinci Code*. Membership of The Magic Circle is taken very seriously and, in keeping with the society's motto (*indocilis private loqui* – "do not speak of private things"), its members are prohibited from revealing the secrets of the craft to anyone other than fellow practitioners. Violators of this sacred principle risk permanent expulsion – for magic cannot exist without mystery.

Entry requirements to The Magic Circle resemble those normally expected of a professional body: candidates must be nominated by two members and pass an interview in which their knowledge and appreciation of magic and the history of magic are carefully assessed. Younger candidates may have to complete a two-year apprenticeship before they can be nominated for membership. Admission to The Magic Circle is only granted once candidates have written an approved thesis or successfully demonstrated their performance skills to a panel of judges in a polished ten-minute magic show. Not even Prince Charles was exempt from this membership requirement – His Royal Highness chose to perform a cup and ball trick for the judges, and the items are displayed in the museum.

The Magic Circle's museum and clubhouse are located in the Centre for the Magic Arts, a sizable building just off the busy Euston Road, which includes a theatre, clubroom, bar, dining room and a 10,000-volume library. The museum is an Alladin's Cave of weird and wonderful artefacts covering every conceivable aspect of the world of magic, not least Harry Houdini's handcuffs.

The Magic Circle Museum, The Centre for the Magic Arts, 12 Stephenson Way, London, NW1 2HD

w: www.themagiccircle.co.uk/about-the-club/ourmuseum
T: +44 (0)20 7841 3600
u: Euston Square
ADMISSION: £

Although the building is normally closed to the public, a two-hour "Magic Circle Experience" tour of the clubhouse and museum can be arranged on selected dates by prior booking. The tour includes a live magic performance and is open to both groups and individuals. Among the highlights is the grand staircase, painted with murals depicting the evolution of the art of magic. For further details please see website.

Above: Classic tricks from the golden age of magic shows
Left: The Magic Circle Museum

The Old Operating Theatre Museum & Herb Garret

In a city noted for its narrow passageways, oddly-shaped buildings and imaginative use of space, quirkily located museums are not unusual in London – but none can be quirkier than an early 19th century operating theatre in the roof of a baroque church.

Accessed via a rickety 32-step spiral staircase (which may prove difficult – or impossible – for the less mobile), Southwark's Old Operating Theatre Museum & Herb Garret is unlike anything else in London and offers a time-travelling experience that is difficult to match. The operating theatre is the oldest in Europe and is located in the garret of St. Thomas's Church (1703), once part of old St. Thomas's Hospital (now relocated to Lambeth). Prior to the installation of the theatre in 1822, the garret was already in use by the hospital's in-house apothecary to store and produce herbal medicines.

The theatre, which hails from an era before anaesthetic, was designed for operations on poor female patients from the adjoining surgical ward of St. Thomas's Hospital, which was located on the same level as the garret, thereby facilitating a smooth transfer of patients to and from the theatre. The tiered seating around the austere operating table complies with the law of the day, which required the attendance of medical and apothecary students at public operations. Despite the obvious indignity, patients would have tolerated the prying eyes, knowing that this enabled them to be seen by the best surgeons in the country and receive treatment that they could never afford.

The herb garret is festooned with all manner of hanging herbs and pickled specimens, as well as eye-watering pre-anaesthetic devices for bleeding, childbirth and trepanning (the drilling of a hole in the skull). Most of the gruesome instruments on display were used primarily for quick operations such as amputations – the lack of antiseptic made internal operations too risky and the lack of anaesthetic necessitated speed: a skilled surgeon could perform an amputation in less than a minute.

Left: The Old Operating Theatre Museum

Above: Pill-making tools in the Herb Garret

Left: The pre-anasthetic operating table with basic instruments and blood-absorbing sawdust at The Old Operating Theatre Museum

The hospital was also used by Florence Nightingale as a site for her famous nursing school, and it was upon her recommendation that the hospital left the area for a new site in 1862. With no hospital on site, the operating theatre and garret were blocked up and remained almost completely forgotten for the next century, until they were rediscovered by a hands-on historian.

Re-enactments of speedy surgical procedures take place in the operating theatre every Saturday at 2pm and demonstrations of herbal medicines take place in the herb garret every Sunday at 2pm. Pre-booking is recommended. Numerous other special events, talks and demonstrations take place during the year.

The Old Operating Theatre Museum and Herb Garret,
9a St. Thomas's Street, London, SE1 9RY
w: www.thegarret.org.uk
t: +44 (0)20 7188 2679
OPEN: Mon–Sun 10:30am–5pm
u: London Bridge
ADMISSION: £

Right: The Petrie Museum of Egyptian Archaeology

The Petrie Museum of Egyptian Archaeology

The Petrie Museum of Egyptian Archaeology is a "must" for all crowd-loathing Egypto-philes. While up to 30,000 people a day can pour in to the British Museum to see the world's second greatest collection of Egyptian antiquities, only a few minutes' walk away, the world's fourth largest collection stands largely ignored – a peaceful oasis affording visitors unobstructed views of exhibits and a calm environment in which they may be appreciated. "Hidden treasure" is a much over-used term but in the case of The Petrie Museum – declared an institution of "outstanding national importance" by the British government – it is well deserved.

Above: A peaceful environment in which to examine Egyptian treasures

The Petrie Museum is part of University College London (UCL) and was established in 1892 to complement the university's newly-founded Department of Egyptian Archaeology. The museum grew to international renown after it acquired the extraordinary collection of artefacts excavated by UCL professor William Petrie (1853–1942) and now includes some 80,000 objects. Moved out of London during the Second World War, the museum has been housed in an old stable building at UCL since the 1950s.

With its old-fashioned display cabinets, The Petrie Museum has the air of a university institution; and this accounts for much of its charm. The museum has not been modernised and it lacks the high-tech interactive features associated with more popular museums – visitors wishing to see darkly lit exhibits more closely can borrow a torch/flashlight from a member of staff.

Museum highlights include the earliest known examples of Egyptian metal, linen, glazing, iron beads and monumental sculpture. The collection also contains treasures from the city of King Akhenaten (the first monotheistic king) and the world's largest collection of mummy portraits.

The Petrie Museum of Egyptian Archaeology, University College London, Malet Place, London, WC1E 6BT
w: www.ucl.ac.uk/museums/petrie
t: +44 (0)20 7679 2884
OPEN: Tue–Sat 1pm–5pm
u: Goodge Street; Euston Square
ADMISSION: Free

The Royal London Hospital Archives and Museum

Before the creation of the National Health Service in 1948, the British population had no automatic health care coverage and it was only the spirit of medical philanthropy and volunteerism that enabled many hospitals to treat the poor and needy. The Royal London Hospital, established in 1740 as the London Infirmary, was once London's largest

Below: The Royal London Hospital Museum

voluntary hospital. In 1748 it was renamed The London Hospital (affectionately known as "The London") before becoming the Royal London Hospital in 1980, following a visit from Queen Elizabeth II. The hospital has existed on its current site in East London's Whitechapel since 1757.

The Royal London Hospital Museum charts the history of the hospital since its foundation and includes features on dentistry, surgery, paediatrics, nursing and the NHS. It is divided by century into three historic periods. The 18th century section includes the hospital charter of 1758, a drawing presented by the artist William Hogarth and George Washington's dentures. The 19th century section features displays about Florence Nightingale and Victorian nursing and special exhibits that focus on key figures and events connected with the institution. Joseph Merrick ("the Elephant Man") lived at the hospital for the last few years of his life, and a display about him includes a model he built of the church and replicas of his hat and veil. The 20th century section includes a display recounting the life of Edith Cavell, the hospital nurse who is nationally celebrated for selflessly saving the lives of soldiers during the First World War without concern for their nationality. She was executed by the Germans after helping 200 soldiers escape from German-occupied Belgium.

An exhibition on forensic medicine includes a feature on Jack the Ripper's Whitechapel murders because Thomas Horrocks Openshaw, the hospital's surgeon and curator, played an important role in the investigation. Artefacts relating to the crimes of Dr. Crippen and John Christie, two of London's most notorious murderers, complete this macabre exhibition.

The Royal London Hospital Archives and Museum reopened after a major refurbishment in 2002 and are housed in the former crypt of St. Philip's, a splendid 19th century church. Visitors may view the main part of the church on weekdays by permission of the Duty Librarian at the reception desk of the Library of the School of Medicine and Dentistry, which is in the same building.

The Royal London Hospital Museum, St. Augustine with Philip's Church, Newark Street, London, E1 2AA
w: www.bartshealth.nhs.uk/rlhmuseum
t: +44 (0)20 7377 7608
open: Sat–Mon closed; Tue–Fri 10am–4:30pm
u: Whitechapel
admission: Free

The museum has a small staff and may close at short notice.
Please check on the day of your visit.

Left: Nurses' uniforms at The Royal London Hospital Museum

Whitechapel Bell Foundry

Does any city have a sound more instantly recognisable than the toll of Big Ben? The mighty bell's unmistakable hourly peal and the familiar Westminster Chime of its sister bells ("All through this hour; Lord, be my guide; And by Thy power; No foot shall slide") are famous throughout the world, immediately conjuring up evocative images of a foggy day in old London town.

Bells have echoed through London's soundscape for centuries. When London was a walled city, church bells rang out the curfew every evening to signal the locking of the city

Below: The Whitechapel Bell Foundry cast Big Ben and the Liberty Bell

Right: Manufacturing one of the bells for The Queen's Diamond Jubilee river pageant in 2012

gates. Traditionally, true cockneys are said to be born within earshot of "Bow Bells", the bells of the church of St. Mary-le-Bow in Cheapside, and generations of children have grown up singing "Oranges and Lemons say the bells of St. Clements", a nursery rhyme identifying the bells of various City churches.

Since 1570 many of London's most important bells have been produced by the Whitechapel Bell Foundry, the oldest manufacturing company in Britain. The Foundry is located on Whitechapel Road in 17th century buildings constructed shortly after the Great Fire of London. The Grade II listed heritage buildings were originally part of a coaching inn named the Artichoke before their conversion into bell-making workshops by the Master Founder of Whitechapel in 1739. In 1752 America's famous Liberty Bell was struck here and just over a century later, in 1858, the Foundry cast Big Ben, its most famous bell. Visitors to the premises walk through a cross section of Big Ben upon entering the front door. Over the centuries, the bells of the Whitechapel Foundry have rung out over cities as far afield as imperial St. Petersburg, Chennai, Washington DC and Toronto.

The historic premises, frozen in time, should not give the impression that the Foundry rests upon past glories. The company continues to manufacture and assemble a wide variety of bells and accessories of assorted shapes and sizes. Given the Foundry's long association with London, it was fitting that it was commissioned to design the special Olympic Bell that rang out at the opening ceremony of London's 2012 Olympic Games, connecting the reign of Queen Elizabeth II with that of Queen Elizabeth I over 400 years earlier. The Olympic Bell is the biggest in Europe and the largest harmonically-tuned bell in the world. Also in 2012, the Foundry cast the bells used in the lead barge at The Queen's Diamond Jubilee river pageant, and which now hang at the City church of St. James Garlickhythe.

The Whitechapel Bell Foundry, 32/35 Whitechapel Road, London, E1 1DY

w: www.whitechapelbellfoundry.co.uk
T: +44 (0)20 7247 2599
U: Whitechapel; Aldgate East

The Foundry's small museum and shop are located in the building foyer and are open to the general public every weekday between 9 am and 5 pm. On selected Saturdays throughout the year individuals and groups may also pre-book a 90-minute guided tour of the Foundry premises.

CHAPTER TWO

SHOPS

From Piccadilly's elegant arcades to Oxford Street's vast department stores, and from Bond Street's luxury boutiques to Hoxton's hip hangouts, London offers some of the world's greatest shopping experiences. This is not a new phenomenon.

In the 19th century, with his mind set to continental domination, Napoleon Bonaparte had dismissed England as little more than "a nation of shopkeepers". The French Emperor may have intended his comment to be derogatory, but there was considerable truth in what he said; so much so, in fact, that England's shopkeepers soon began to quote the Emperor's insult with pride. England was and is a nation of shopkeepers, and London is its undisputed shopping capital.

More than 200 years after Napoleon's bombast, the humble London shopkeeper may be forgiven for feeling slightly smug – for whilst Napoleon is now a distant memory, many of the shops that existed during his lifetime continue to thrive. To this day, it is still possible to purchase a hat from the shop that made the famous bicorn worn by the Duke of Wellington when he defeated Napoleon at the Battle of Waterloo.

Few walks are finer for the historically-minded shopper than the short stroll from the home of the suit (Savile Row) through the world's first shopping arcade (Burlington Arcade) and down to the bottom of St. James's Street, passing in quick succession the world's oldest

Left: The best of British: An officer and a guardsman shopping in exclusive St. James's

bootmaker (John Lobb), tobacconist (James J. Fox of St. James Ltd.), hat shop (Lock & Co.), barbershop (Truefitt & Hill) and Britain's oldest wine and spirit merchant (Berry Bros. & Rudd).

Enduring through the ages, these shops and a few other London survivors have come to symbolise the adage "Business As Usual", the defiant motto famously popularised during the Second World War, when bombing razed much of the city to the ground. Yet, whilst these shops retain an atmospheric old-world charm, their continued success rests on their ability to satisfy the demands of the modern customer, and offer products and services of the highest quality.

Left: The north wall of Berry Bros. & Rudd (allegedly part of Henry VIII's tennis court) and the alleyway leading to Pickering Place, the smallest public square in England and the site of the country's last public duel

Right: Berry Bros. & Rudd

Berry Bros. & Rudd
A DIPLOMATIC AFFAIR

Berry Bros. & Rudd is Britain's oldest wine and spirit merchant and has traded from the same shop at No. 3 St. James's Street since 1698, making it one of the world's oldest *in situ* companies. To put its age in context, the shop started trading as a grocer's, a mere five years after the end of the Salem witch trials in colonial Massachusetts. The building certainly looks ancient: its elegant façade is caked in centuries of paint, and the immaculate, almost entirely wooden interior is so close to an idealised depiction of an 18th century shop that one might be forgiven for thinking it had been purchased from a Hollywood set designer.

Above: The main floor of Berry Bros. & Rudd, including the famous weighing scales

Long before it was used for commercial purposes, the site functioned as King Henry VIII's real tennis court, part of which allegedly survives to this day as the shop's north wall. The wall runs the length of Pickering Passage, the alleyway that connects St. James's Street with Pickering Place, itself worthy of note as the smallest public square in England and reputedly the scene of the country's last duel.

Little is known about the shop's founder other than that she was called the Widow Bourne, she had at least two daughters and she wisely chose to locate her grocers' shop opposite St. James's Palace in the year that it became the principal official residence of the Monarchy (1698 – the Palace of Whitehall having burned down in January of the same year).

By the end of the 17th century the neighbourhood of St. James's was already prestigious and the Widow and her family were quick to supply coffee to the area's newly-fashionable coffee houses, forerunners of St. James's private gentlemen's clubs. The most obvious relics of the shop's earlier incarnation must be the famous large coffee mill and huge weighing scales

Right: Plaque commemorating the legation of the Republic of Texas

that dominate the main floor. By 1765 the shop had become well-known for weighing people, a tradition that continues to this day (albeit not as frequently). Famous figures listed in the shop's weighing books include royalty, Lord Byron, Beau Brummell and William Pitt the Younger.

Even today, although its coffee days are long gone and its business is limited to fine wine and spirits, Berry Bros. & Rudd continues to trade under "The Sign of the Coffee Mill", a sign that hung outside the shop for centuries.

Below ground level, Berry Bros. & Rudd boasts secret passageways (one of which is alleged to connect the shop to St. James's Palace) and immense cellars, once the largest working cellars in London. Demonstrating the company's ability to adapt with the times, parts of the cellars have recently been converted into entertaining spaces for wine classes and private parties. Despite the conversions, the cellars still hold approximately 100,000 bottles of wine. During his exile from France in the 1840s, a friend of George Berry named Prince Louis Napoleon (later Emperor Napoleon III), plotted his return to France from a section of the cellars now appropriately renamed the "Napoleon Cellar".

Remarkably, this wasn't the only involvement the shop had in international affairs during that decade: from 1842–1845 Berry Bros. & Rudd housed the legation of the independent Republic of Texas to the Court of St. James's. The Texas Legation's historic presence is commemorated by two plaques on the wall of Pickering Place – one erected in 1963 and another dedicated by Governor Rick Perry of Texas in 2013.

Berry Bros. & Rudd, 3 St. James's Street, London, SW1A 1EG

w: www.bbr.com

t: +44 (0)20 7022 8973

u: Green Park

Henry Poole & Co.
HOME OF THE DINNER JACKET

The modern suit may have evolved into three distinct English, Italian and American styles, but it was born in London. Ever since, the city's tailors have successfully maintained London's status as a capital of classic men's fashion, with Savile Row, long synonymous with bespoke suits and traditional gentlemen's tailoring, a site of pilgrimage for suit lovers. Such is the apotheosis of "the global mile of tailoring" (as this short stretch of the street is known), that the Japanese word for suit is "sabiro", a corrupted version of "Savile Row". Even the word "bespoke" is said to have originated in Savile Row, dating to a time when valuable suit cloth was said to "be spoken for" by specific customers.

On a street defined by status, rivalry is intense and precedence difficult to rank. Yet it is not too controversial to suggest that by virtue of its longevity, history and distinguished clientele, Henry Poole & Co., an original founder of Savile Row and birthplace of the dinner jacket, is the grand doyen of Savile Row tailoring.

The company was founded by James Poole in Bloomsbury in 1806, was moved to Savile Row by his son Henry in 1846 and remains under family ownership. At around the time of the move to Savile Row, to the good fortune of Henry Poole & Co., Prince Louis Napoleon (later Emperor Napoleon III) became the company's first royal customer, having transposed himself to London following his exile from France. In 1858, a few years after ascending the French throne, the Emperor granted the shop its first royal warrant, another 40 would follow. To this day, Napoleon III's coat of arms hangs in the shop window, along with those of Queen Elizabeth II and the late Emperor Haile Selassie of Ethiopia.

By the 1870s Henry Poole & Co. was the tailor of choice for so many European royal households that it became the obvious candidate to produce accurate copies of royal uniforms for Madame Tussaud's famous Wax Museum on Marylebone Road. A working relationship between the two institutions was established and Henry Poole & Co. found itself in the slightly unusual position of producing clothes for both living customers and their wax models. Regrettably, the majority of these latter garments were destroyed in a major fire at Madame Tussaud's in 1925.

Henry Poole & Co's most important contribution to fashion is undoubtedly the creation of the dinner jacket, also known as the tuxedo. Today the dinner jacket is regarded as formal

Right: Henry Poole & Co.

attire, however when the achingly fashionable Prince of Wales (later Edward VII) approached Poole & Co in 1860 to design a new evening garment, it was because he wanted an outfit considerably less formal than the stiff "white tie and tails" evening dress that was the standard dress code of the era. The tailless dinner jacket was a radical (and socially shocking) departure from accepted norms, and the Prince of Wales wore it frequently while dining informally with friends at Sandringham, his country retreat. Seen by a member (or members) of the exclusive Tuxedo Club of New York state, the jacket was brought to America, where its popularity spread far beyond the club whose name it now bears.

The dinner jacket has become an iconic fashion item and a byword for sophistication, entrenched in popular culture through global icons such as Frank Sinatra and legendary characters such as Ian Fleming's James Bond. Walking past the small shop front, few passers-by can imagine how influential Henry Poole & Co. has been.

Henry Poole & Co., 15 Savile Row, London, W1S 3PJ

w: www.henrypoole.com
T: +44 (0)20 7734 5985
U: Piccadilly Circus

Above: The expert tailors of Henry Poole & Co.

Right: Items from James J. Fox's museum, including the chair used by Sir Winston Churchill

James J. Fox
CHURCHILL'S CHOICE

Parliament may have banned smoking in work places and enclosed public spaces but London retains a tiny number of oases where the sampling of handmade cigars is still permitted – and No. 19 St. James's Street is perhaps the most special. Not only is this handsome shop the world's oldest cigar merchant, it was also Sir Winston Churchill's preferred supplier for over 60 years – and customers would be denying themselves one of London's truly unique experiences if they did not ask to sample Churchill's favourite brand of cigar from the well-worn chair in which he sat. The small in-house museum, which is free of charge and open during shop hours, is another of London's best kept secrets and can be enjoyed by smokers and non-smokers alike.

London is not short of beautifully-preserved interiors but, through the aroma of fine tobacco, James J. Fox provides the additional atmospheric element that others now lack. The effect is pleasant and far from overpowering; and visitors need not fear exposure to billowing clouds of smoke – cigar smoking is relegated to an upstairs room some distance from the shop floor. Cigars may be enjoyed at James J. Fox because it is a specialist merchant, however the smoking ban exemption is very limited: cigars must be purchased on site and are smoked on the understanding that customers are sampling the products with a view to purchasing more.

A fine tobacconist has occupied 19 St. James's Street since Robert Lewis Ltd. finally settled there in the 1840s. Founded by Christopher Lewis in Covent Garden in 1787, Robert Lewis operated for over 200 years until it was acquired by James J. Fox in 1992. Ever since, and with the active participation of the fifth generation of the Fox family, the two united companies have traded under the name J.J. Fox (St. James's) Ltd.

The shop's small museum was originally located in an intimate room in the basement, but the contents have been temporarily dispersed around the ground floor, where they afford a fascinating glimpse into the world of the cigar aficionado. Entering an imposing shop in a prestigious location can be intimidating, but there is no need for trepidation: staff members at James J. Fox are very friendly, and those wishing to view the exhibits are under no obligation to purchase goods. Notable items on display include the oldest box of Havana cigars in the world (made for the Great Exhibition of 1851), royal warrants and a High Court letter to settle the shop account of the bankrupt Oscar Wilde (whose cigarettes were individually inscribed 'Oscar' in red ink).

However it is the association with Sir Winston Churchill that the shop celebrates most. An entire display cabinet in the museum is dedicated to Churchill-related artefacts ("Churchilliana"), and small plaster statues of Sir Winston may even be purchased at the till. The world's best-known cigar smoker made his first purchase at No. 19 St. James's Street in August 1900, when he was 25. Although Churchill bought from various cigar merchants over the course of his life (with each one keen to boast of the connection), there is no doubting Churchill's long-standing preference for Robert Lewis (as the shop was then known). The business ledgers and letters on display testify to the longevity of this relationship, which continued until Churchill's death some 65 years after his first purchase.

James J. Fox, 19 St. James's Street, London, SW1A 1ES

w: www.jjfox.co.uk

t: +44 (0)20 7930 3787

u: Green Park

Right: The helpful staff of James J. Fox

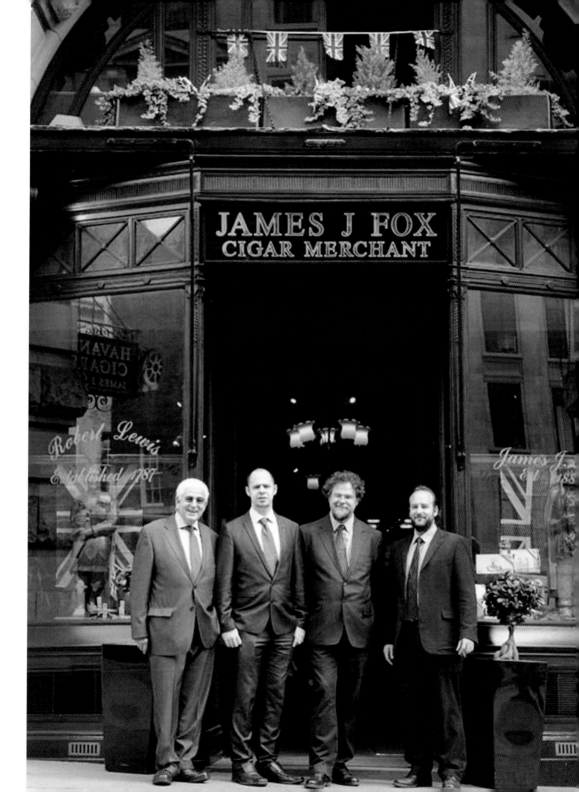

James Smith & Sons
QUINTESSENTIALLY LONDON

Few cities' residents are as instantly identifiable as the bowler-hatted Londoner carrying a tightly-rolled umbrella. The image may be outdated – and the mobile phone may have supplanted the umbrella as the indispensable item of London life – yet for generations of Londoner a "brolly" was almost a fifth limb, as vital to a daily commuter as a spear to a

Above and Left: The timeless interior and protected façade of James Smith & Sons

Massai warrior. As the unofficial home of the umbrella, it is fitting that London is the location of James Smith & Sons, an umbrella emporium without equal – the oldest in Europe, and probably the grandest in the world.

Established in 1830 and operating out of the same building on New Oxford Street since 1857, James Smith & Sons has barely changed in over 180 years. Now as then, master craftsmen operate from a workshop on the premises to design, manufacture and repair umbrellas and walking sticks. The shop itself is a perfectly-preserved Victorian gem, boasting one of London's most unforgettable shop fronts. In 1999 the building received official heritage listing to protect its original exterior signage and interior showroom; however it is inconceivable that anyone could ever consider altering this palace of parasols. Entering the entrancingly cluttered shop, almost every inch used for display space, is to step into another, slightly magical, world. If Mary Poppins needed a new umbrella, or Harry Potter another wand, James Smith & Sons is where they would come.

James Smith & Sons, 53 New Oxford Street, London, WC1A 1BL
w: www.james-smith.co.uk
t: +44 (0)20 7836 4731
u: Tottenham Court Road

John Lobb
"THE MOST BEAUTIFUL SHOP IN THE WORLD"

Of the commercial establishments encountered on St. James's Street, perhaps none has had a more famous or illustrious clientele than John Lobb, bootmaker to royalty, politicians and celebrities since 1866. Everything about this exquisite shop exudes grandeur and sophistication. No. 9 St. James's Street, within the shadow of St. James's Palace and surrounded by London's most exclusive private gentlemen's clubs, could hardly be a better location for a bootmaker. Located on the site of Lord Byron's bachelor apartment, even its geographic pedigree is impeccable. The shop's interior (albeit rebuilt following Second World War bomb damage) was sufficiently impressive for Esquire magazine to dub it "...the most beautiful shop in the world".

The company's origins are humble. In the mid-19th century John Lobb, the crippled son of a Cornish farmer, journeyed to London to become an apprentice to an established city bootmaker. Lobb travelled to Australia soon after finishing his apprenticeship, to make hollow-heeled boots for gold rush prospectors – the hollow heels providing a secure space in which to safely store gold nuggets. After winning medals in London's International Exhibition of 1862, Lobb sent a pair of shoes to The Prince of Wales (later King Edward VII). The Prince was so impressed by the quality of the workmanship that he commissioned Lobb to supply his personal footwear, bestowing his royal warrant soon after. Having received the ultimate seal of approval, Lobb set up his shop on St. James's Street in 1866.

Where kings tread, the rich and powerful soon follow. Over the past century and a half, John Lobb has provided its bespoke services to a glittering array of royalty, politicians, business tycoons, actors, writers and musicians. Treating each pair of handmade shoes like a work of art, John Lobb's craftsmen never forget that they are practitioners of "the gentle craft" (as shoemaking is known). Remarkably, all historic shoe "lasts" – wooden models of the contours of clients' feet – are tagged and stored in Lobb's basement, usually with descriptive notes.

In 2009 The Prince of Wales and The Duchess of Cornwall honoured Lobb with a royal visit. The thousands of shoe lasts they saw on the racks resembled a wooden *Who's Who*. Taken together, the lasts provide perhaps the oddest juxtaposition of names in London: Queen Victoria, Frank Sinatra, Enrico Caruso, Laurence Olivier, George Bernard Shaw, Duke Ellington and Andy Warhol (to name but a few). Perhaps only here can one discover that

Right: The interior of John Lobb Ltd.

Above: Shoe lasts in the basement of John Lobb Ltd.

Jackie Kennedy had a larger shoe size than her husband Aristotle Onassis, or that the Duke of Windsor had "rather bony feet". Naturally, such personalised service comes at a price – but anyone with such concerns has probably come to the wrong place.

John Lobb, 9 St. James's Street, London, SW1A 1EF
w: www.johnlobbltd.co.uk
t: +44 (0)20 7930 3664
u: Green Park

Lock & Co.
THE WORLD'S OLDEST HATTER

Standing outside this small but venerable building at No. 6 St. James's Street, its crooked doorway contorted by the centuries, few would be surprised to learn that this is both the world's oldest hat shop and one of its oldest family-owned businesses.

Since 1676, the hats of James Lock & Co. have adorned the heads of tens of thousands, amongst them many historical figures, not least legendary hat-lovers Admiral Lord Nelson, Sir Winston Churchill and Charlie Chaplin. The windows of the perfectly-preserved shop front have borne silent witness to countless evolutions in millinery style and fashion, yet Lock & Co. remains an insider's institution – unknown to most Londoners, save those who need to know. Ask any London taxi driver to take you to "Lock's", and without fail you will be driven to St. James's Street. Upon your arrival, the shop's dedicated employees will need little prompting to recount the story of the postcard that arrived safely despite bearing no address other than "the best hatters in the world, London."

Right: Lock & Co.

Left: A traditional device for heads and hat sizes at Lock & Co.

A favourite with the upper classes and the holder of two royal warrants (as hatters to The Prince of Wales and The Duke of Edinburgh), Lock & Co. can even lay claim to the creation of the definitive symbol of the British establishment: the bowler hat. But beware: any man seeking to purchase such a hat in order to join the higher ranks would be off to a very bad start if he walked in here to ask for a "bowler". At Lock & Co. a bowler hat is called a "Coke" (pronounced "cook") – and as they were the first to sell it, they can surely call it what they wish.

The coke is named after Edward Coke, younger brother of the Earl of Leicester, for whom the hat was first made in 1849. Lock & Co. commissioned London hat designers Thomas and William Bowler to create a short, well-fitting hard hat that could be worn by Coke's game keepers for protection from tree branches whilst on horseback (a top hat being impractical). Arriving at Lock & Co. to inspect the new hat, Coke allegedly put it on the shop floor and stamped on it twice to test its strength. Today's customers would be advised not to try this until after they have completed their purchase!

Lock & Co., 6 St. James's Street, London, SW1A 1EF
w: www.lockhatters.co.uk
t: +44 (0)20 7930 8874
u: Green Park

Paxton & Whitfield
THE QUEEN'S CHEESEMONGER

Jermyn Street is globally renowned for its traditional shirtmakers and retailers of gentlemen's accessories. A short stroll past the area's numerous clothiers will leave no one doubting the motto: "Suits from Savile Row, Shirts from Jermyn Street". To stumble upon a cheese shop in the middle of such an exclusive address may seem odd; but this is no ordinary cheesemonger – Paxton & Whitfield is the country's most prestigious purveyor of cheese and has been the height of fashion since the 19th century.

Paxton & Whitfield's earliest record as a partnership dates back to 1797 (although its origins date back half a century earlier, to 1742). However incongruous it may now appear, the family-owned company has been located around Jermyn Street since the early 19th century and predates all of the district's famous shirtmakers. Paxton & Whitfield's reputation for excellence was firmly established in 1850, when it received a Royal Warrant from Queen Victoria. More than 160 years and several royal warrants later, Queen Elizabeth II, Victoria's great-great-granddaughter, continues the company's royal connection. Cheese from this small shop is personally delivered to Buckingham Palace – by the trade entrance, of course.

Paxton & Whitfield, 93 Jermyn Street, London, SW1Y 6JE
W: www.paxtonandwhitfield.co.uk
T: +44 (0)20 7930 0259
U: Piccadilly Circus

Right: Paxton & Whitfield

Truefitt & Hill
THE WORLD'S OLDEST BARBERSHOP

In 1805, while Lord Nelson sailed the seas to engage the French fleet at the Battle of Trafalgar, an entrepreneur named William Francis Truefitt established himself in Mayfair as a barber, wigmaker and perfumer. Truefitt's timing could not have been better. The early 19th century was the golden age of the "dandy", vain gentlemen devoted to little more than leisure, grooming and personal appearance. Wigs, which had long been *de rigeur* for gentlemen, were falling out of favour with the fashionable, not least because of the *Duty on Hair Powder Act 1795*, which sought to tax hair and wig powder in order to raise funds for the Napoleonic wars – as well as to discourage the frivolous use of flour at a time of national shortage. When Beau Brummell, the era's foremost dandy and arbiter of taste, chose to have his hair styled "a la Brutus", the fashion for haircuts was set.

Below: Early premises of Truefitt & Hill at Burlington Arcade

Above: Current premises of Truefitt & Hill, next to the Carlton Club

Truefitt's exceptional products and services soon established the shop as a world leader in men's grooming, so much so that it is even mentioned in the novels of two regular customers: William Makepeace Thackeray and Charles Dickens. Since the time of King George III, through nine consecutive reigns, Truefitt has served the Royal Family and has benefitted from the custom of famous figures such as Oscar Wilde, Alfred Hitchcock, Frank Sinatra and Cary Grant. In 1935 Truefitt acquired the hairdressing business of Edwin S. Hill & Co., thus becoming Truefitt & Hill. The shop moved to its present location next to the historic Carlton Club on St. James's Street in 1994.

Today Truefitt & Hill's royal associations continue, and it proudly displays a royal warrant from The Duke of Edinburgh above the main entrance. However, customers waiting for a traditional wet shave will be disappointed if they expect to find themselves sitting next to The Queen's husband – barbers from the shop are required to attend to The Duke in private at Buckingham Palace or Windsor Castle. Nevertheless, other members of the royal family, as well as celebrities and distinguished personalities, regularly visit the elegant St. James's Street premises for a haircut or to purchase grooming supplies or fragrances. In April 2000 *The Guinness Book of World Records* officially recognised Truefitt & Hill as the world's oldest barbershop.

Truefitt & Hill, 71 St. James's Street, London, SW1A 1PH
w: www.truefittandhill.co.uk
t: +44 (0)20 7493 8496
u: Green Park

IN THE FOOTSTEPS
OF JAMES BOND

Not since that other intrepid Londoner Sherlock Holmes, has a fictional character become as ingrained in popular culture as Ian Fleming's James Bond. When the dashing spy is not saving the world from Armageddon or battling enemies of the state in distant lands, James Bond is very much the man about London town. The relationship between London and James Bond is almost symbiotic: London features prominently in the Bond novels and films while Bond played a leading role in the opening ceremony of the 2012 London Olympics, meeting The Queen at Buckingham Palace and famously jumping out of a helicopter with Her Majesty above the Olympic Stadium.

Admirers of 007s effortless sophistication and unerring sense of style flock to London to immerse themselves in all things Bond. If you wish to dress, drink or dine like the suave spy, this is your guide.

MARTINI

A dry martini "shaken not stirred" may be the most famous drink order in the history of film and is no doubt repeated to weary barmen across the world every evening. If James Bond were to choose any bar in London to order his favourite martini today, many believe he would opt for the legendary bar at Duke's Hotel in St. James's. Bond creator Ian Fleming was a patron of Duke's Bar and its martinis are internationally renowned – their potency is so great that to avoid seeing double (or 007!) patrons are restricted to no more than three per visit.

The barman at Duke's is almost as legendary as the bar itself and, in celebration of the Bond connection, he has partnered with Floris, the nearby perfumery whose "89" Eau de Cologne was a favourite of Ian Fleming's, to create a new martini: the Fleming 89. Sipping martinis in the plush surroundings and rarefied atmosphere of this intimate venue, it is easy to imagine Bond settling in to his favourite seat accompanied by yet another improbably named femme fatale.

After a martini or two at Duke's it is only a short stroll to Scott's restaurant in Mayfair, a favourite haunt of Ian Fleming since his days at the Admiralty (where Commander Bond's career started). Now on Mount Street, in Fleming's day the restaurant was located on Coventry Street and is thought to be where Bond dined on dressed crab. If the phrase "shaken not stirred" was not coined at Duke's Bar, it may well have originated at Scott's.

LEISURE

In addition to Duke's and Scott's, several other establishments can lay claim to bona fide 007 connections. Bond's lifestyle is almost inseparable from that of Ian Fleming, and where Fleming went Bond was sure to follow. The Savoy Hotel's famous American Bar and Savoy Grill were both regular ports of call for Fleming and the hotel is mentioned in a few Bond novels. In 2012, to celebrate the launch of *Carte Blanche*, a new Bond novel by American writer Jeffrey Deaver, the American Bar introduced a specially-created "Carte Blanche" cocktail. It is served alongside the "Vesper", a Bond variation on the martini, first mentioned in *Casino Royale*.

Blade's Club is the fictional private gentlemen's club of which James Bond's boss "M", Head of the Secret Intelligence Service, is a member and which Bond visited on several occa-

Left: Duke's Bar at Duke's Hotel

Above: The Savoy Hotel

Below: Boodle's

sions. The club is partly modelled on Fleming's own club, Boodle's (28 St. James's Street), and is located around the corner from it, on the fictional Park Street (in reality Park Place), close to Pratt's club (14 Park Place).

GROOMING

Geo. F. Trumper is a traditional London barber that has been pampering well-heeled gentlemen in Mayfair since 1875. Trumper's "Eucris" eau de toilette is mentioned in the James Bond novels and it is reasonable to assume that if Bond shopped in the elegant premises on Curzon Street, he would almost certainly have stayed for a shave and a haircut. Trumper's "Eucris" eau de toilette, soaps and shaving creams are available from the company's two locations on Curzon Street and Duke of York Street.

Floris has been a family perfumer since Juan Famenias Floris and his wife started selling fragrances and shaving products from 89 Jermyn Street in 1730. The shop has remained at the same location, and in the same family, ever since and is the proud holder of two royal

Below: Geo. F. Trumper, Curzon Street

warrants. Floris is mentioned in three James Bond novels (*Moonraker, Diamonds Are Forever* and *Dr. No*) and Ian Fleming enjoyed wearing Floris' fragrance No. 89, which takes its name from the shop's street number.

SUITS

Sean Connery was the first actor to play James Bond on the big screen and it was his early films that set the style and tone for the now unmistakable Bond brand. Much of the credit for the spy's image is due to the attention to detail of Terence Young, the well-dressed director of the first Bond films. Young engaged his personal tailor, Anthony Sinclair, to create Connery's suits in the first Bond film, *Dr. No*, and Sinclair continued to produce suits for the next four productions: *From Russia With Love, Goldfinger, You Only Live Twice* and *Diamonds are Forever*. According to Sinclair, the young and largely unknown Sean Connery was not naturally comfortable in suits so Terrence Young instructed Connery to get used to them by wearing them around the clock, including in bed!

Fittings at Anthony Sinclair's Montagu Square premises are by appointment only, but for those seeking the Bond look without paying £2,000 for a suit, Anthony Sinclair has embraced the age of the Internet and now produces a replica of Bond's cavalry twill trousers, as featured in *Goldfinger*. In 2014, to mark the production of *Bond 24*, Anthony Sinclair launched a knitted tie collection available in 24 colours, harking back to the ties worn by Connery in the early films.

SHIRTS

In the film series, James Bond is most frequently seen wearing shirts made by Frank Foster and Turnbull & Asser, two exclusive shirtmakers globally recognised as masters of the bespoke shirt experience. Frank Foster has discreetly dressed the most famous men in the world for more than sixty years and sees no need for a fancy website. Fittings at No. 40 Pall Mall are by appointment only. The great Orson Welles, a regular customer, once sent for Frank Foster whilst staying at the Savoy Hotel. Foster politely declined, sending a message back to Welles informing the legendary actor that he would find it was the same distance from the Savoy to his premises.

Turnbull & Asser is considerably more accessible, with a flagship shop on Jermyn Street, branches in the City and New York, and a fully interactive on-line store. The company has a long association with the royal family and currently holds a Royal Warrant from The Prince of Wales, who even asked the company to design a tailored sling after he broke his arm playing polo.

Left: Floris, Jermyn Street

Right: Frank Foster: London's most discreet retailer?

Below: Turnbull & Asser, Jermyn Street

Turnbull & Asser has made shirts for four Bond actors as well as for author Ian Fleming and director Terrence Young. In addition to its bespoke shirts (minimum order of six), Turnbull & Asser also produces ready-to-wear shirts and accessories, and recently launched a James Bond range, including Bond ties, "The *Casino Royale* dress shirt" and "The *Dr. No* shirt".

Above: John Lobb Ltd.

SHOES

Ian Fleming and Sean Connery were both customers of John Lobb Ltd. and it is safe to assume that, given his eye for quality, James Bond would have owned at least one pair of shoes from this grand shoemaker. Although all of Lobb's shoes are bespoke, Bond aficionados probably shouldn't ask for a pair containing a hidden knife, as worn by the character Rosa Klebb in *From Russia With Love*! A longer entry on John Lobb Ltd. appears on page 54.

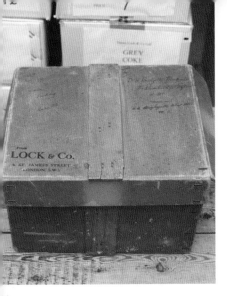

HATS

The trilby worn by Sean Connery in the first James Bond film was supplied by Lock & Co., and a version is still available for sale today. In the 1989 film *Licence to Kill*, Bond actor Timothy Dalton wore a grey top hat from Lock & Co., although it wasn't long until it had been shot by a bullet. A full entry on Lock & Co., the oldest hatshop in the world, appears on page 57.

ACCESSORIES

Above: An old Lock & Co. hatbox

As any Bond fan should know, Q-branch, the division of MI6 that produced 007's ingenious gadgets, issued all "00" agents with a red-lined black leather Swaine Adeney Brigg attaché case. The case was mentioned in the novel *From Russia With Love* and played a prominent role in the film version, saving Bond's life on more than one occasion. The capacious case concealed a host of "must have" espionage items which no self-respecting spy would be seen dead without (literally!).

The SAB Bond 4.5" case remains a popular item with collectors and enthusiasts and although the £2,000 modern replicas may not include a strip of gold coins, rounds of ammunition, throwing knives and a folding rifle, they can be modified to each customer's specific needs.

Swaine Adeney Brigg was founded in 1750 and is a distinguished leather luggage and umbrella retailer that holds royal warrants from both The Queen and The Prince of Wales. Coincidentally, the company is also known for making bespoke luggage for owners of Aston Martin cars, another brand intimately associated with James Bond.

007's attaché case isn't Swaine Adeney Brigg's only claim to film fame: when producing *Raiders of the Lost Ark*, the first film in the Indiana Jones trilogy, director Stephen Spielberg found Indiana Jones's now iconic brown felt hat at Swaine Adeney Brigg. Ironically, James Bond was the inspiration for the Indiana Jones character – which is why Sean Connery was cast as Jones' father in the third film of the trilogy. The company has occupied several locations in the St. James's area and is now located in the Piccadilly Arcade.

WORK

Until the construction of the immense fortress-like building at Vauxhall Cross on the South Bank of the River Thames in 1994, Britain's Secret Intelligence Service's presence in London was suitably mysterious. In his novels Ian Fleming placed the organisation on the eighth floor

Above: Piccadilly Arcade, home to Swaine Adeney Brigg.

of the Ministry of Works near Regent's Park whilst the films have set it in a number of locations, including an office block at the corner of Trafalgar Square and Pall Mall (57 Trafalgar Square) and the Old War Office building in Whitehall. Since the film *Goldeneye* in 1995, the actual Secret Intelligence Service Headquarters in Vauxhall has featured prominently in the Bond series. The building is closed to the public but fans of 007 will get a good view from the riverside and from Vauxhall Bridge.

Below: Britain's Secret Intelligence Service (MI6) Headquarters at Vauxhall Cross.

CHAPTER THREE

HOUSES

There should be no surprise that it was a Londoner (the jurist Sir Edward Coke) who coined the famous adage: "a man's house is his castle". The London house is as much a statement as a building and has long symbolised the sober values and beliefs traditionally associated with the British people: privacy, individualism, capitalism, law and order. Until London property prices made it prohibitively expensive, house ownership traditionally set inhabitants of the British capital apart from the residents of other large European cities. Londoners owned houses and relaxed in private gardens, Parisians rented apartments and socialised in public squares.

Left: The drawing room of Dennis Severs' House

London's historic houses offer the clearest insight into the city's social and architectural history, and provide the best window into the immense variety of life that has existed in the capital through the ages. Until time travel is invented, houses are the next best thing.

The majority of London's historic houses are notable because of their famous residents or their architecture, and sometimes both. The result is a wide range of houses scattered across all areas of the city, reflecting very different histories and hugely varied styles of building, decoration and interior design.

London's architecture is far less homogeneous than in most comparable great cities. As London grew, it engulfed many old and diverse villages and settlements, a number of which retained their distinctive character long after becoming suburban boroughs. The result is a sprawling metropolis that encompasses hilltop cottages, riverside terraces, marshland houses and grand city palaces.

The best preserved and most visited houses invariably belong to the rich and famous; this can skew our perception of the past and inaccurately romanticise earlier eras. It is only through efforts to preserve and restore more commonplace domestic architecture that London has been able to tell its fuller story. The lesser-known, and barely known, houses featured in this section reflect a range of historical, social and architectural diversity almost as broad as that of the city itself.

London's Smallest Houses

Buckingham Palace is London's largest home but, at the other end of the spectrum, the capital's smallest house is more difficult to identify. Some of the city's quirkiest homes are so oddly shaped that over the years more than one property has been unofficially described as the smallest or narrowest in London. One thing is certain: although London's smallest houses may be tiny, their price tags aren't. Located in some of the world's most prestigious postcodes, any one of these miniscule abodes could be sold to purchase a substantial property outside the city.

At a metre in width, No. 10 Hyde Park Place was long considered the best contender for the title of "London's smallest house". The first property built here was constructed in 1805, seemingly to block a narrow alleyway that provided access to the nearby burial ground at St. George's Fields. In the 18th and 19th centuries, body snatchers earned their living from the dead: stealing recently deceased corpses and selling them to anatomists for anatomical research. The macabre trade was such a problem that many churches and cemeteries had little option but to hire night watchmen to apprehend or deter these sacrilegious "resurrectionists", as body snatchers were then known. The original tiny building that occupied this site was most likely used by a watchman, perhaps as both a home and a watch tower.

An equally minute house replaced the original building later in the 19th century but records note only one tenant (the writer and producer Lewis George Wallace, d. 2002). The house suffered some bomb damage during the Second World War and it was eventually replaced with the tiny modern structure that stands on the site today. As the current building is now incorporated into the adjacent Tyburn Convent, it is probably no longer accurate to describe it as a "house".

In December 2009 Britain's tabloids, in their inimitable fashion, proclaimed that "the narrowest house in London" was on sale for approximately half a million pounds – claustrophobics need not apply. With over 1,000 square feet spread over five floors, the three bedroomed house located at 110 Goldhawk Road is not tiny, but at a width of just over 1.5 metres its extreme skinniness is beyond doubt. Interior photographs of the house in trendy Shepherd's Bush showed opposing walls that could be touched by outstretched arms and a bed that could only be accessed from its foot. This sliver of a building was built in the 1870s

Left: No. 10 Hyde Park Place

to fill a space next to a grocer's shop and over the years it has been home to several artists, perhaps most notably fashion photographer Jurgen Teller.

Whilst the media continue to promote 110 Goldhawk Road as London's skinniest house, an even thinner and more unusual London property has passed largely unnoticed. 1 Ennismore Gardens Mews is a former stable building located in exclusive Knightsbridge. "Mews" is a traditional term for a row of small stables (usually with living quarters above) used to service nearby, often adjoining, grand houses – the stables were the historical equivalent of the modern garage. As horses disappeared from London's streets, the hodge podge of quirky stable buildings in the city's numerous mews were gradually converted into private residences, becoming some of London's most desirable and expensive homes.

What function 1 Ennismore Gardens Mews originally served is not known – it couldn't even house a miniature pony – but this long, single-storey building no more than a metre in width has been a private home for many years.

10 Hyde Park Place W2 2LJ, 110 Goldhawk Road W12 8HD and 1 Ennismore Gardens Mews SW7 1HX are private residences that are not open to the public.

Left: No. 110 Goldhawk Road   *Above:* No. 1 Ennismore Gardens Mews

London's Oldest House

London's antiquity is not always obvious. The Great Fire of 1666, aerial bombardment during the Second World War and the destruction of vast swathes of the city by "progressive" 19th and 20th century urban planners have erased much of London's historic core. Aside from the City of London's medieval street pattern and street names, and the occasional roman or medieval crypt, there is relatively little to suggest that the city's famous "Square Mile", the financial hub of modern London, is also its 2,000 year old heart.

Fortunately, the Square Mile continues to offer a few tantalising glimpses of the London that used to be. One tiny corner that emerged relatively unscathed from the onslaught of the ages can be found in Farringdon, around St. Bartholomew's Hospital, one of the oldest working hospitals in the world. Hidden in this network of cosy nooks is No. 41–42 Cloth Fair, the oldest house in London and the only remaining City dwelling to have escaped the Great Fire.

Completed before 1614, this beautiful house was spared destruction in the Great Fire due to its position behind the wall of a former 12th century Augustinian priory. The priory was dissolved by Henry VIII in 1539 but the ancient priory Church of St. Bartholomew the Great remains to this day. One of London's oldest religious buildings, St. Bartholomew the Great is perhaps best known for featuring in films such as *Four Weddings and a Funeral*, *Shakespeare in Love* and *Elizabeth: The Golden Age*.

Given Henry VIII's responsibility for dissolving the ancient priory, it may seem odd that the gatehouse of St. Bartholomew's Hospital should feature his only public statue in London, but it is not as strange as it first seems. The dissolution of the priory had left the hospital in such a precarious financial position that King Henry refounded the hospital, granting it lands and income to support its good work. The priory's loss was the hospital's gain, and the statue of King Henry VIII acknowledges his charity.

For several centuries cloth merchants gathered in Cloth Fair to market their wares at the internationally famous Bartholomew Fair, held here from 1133 to 1855. By the late 17th century the original textile fair had expanded to include a wide range of side shows, including prize fighters, acrobats, freak shows and exotic animals. The poet William Wordsworth found the fair so remarkable that he wrote about it at some length, noting in particular the "Horse of

Right: The Tudor Gatehouse of the Church of St. Bartholomew the Great

Above: The Church of St. Bartholomew the Great

Knowledge" and the famous "Learned Pig", an animal renowned for telling the time to the nearest minute – an impressive act apparently made more difficult because it was blind-folded! The fair's reputation for debauchery and public disorder caused it to be shut down by the City in 1855.

With its weatherboards and wooden projecting window, the expertly restored No. 41–42 Cloth Fair is a fine example of a Jacobean town house and it received the City Heritage Award in 2000 for contributing to the enhancement of the environment of the City of London. Prior to their unnecessary demolition in 1917, many pre Great Fire houses stood on Cloth Fair and No. 41–42 might have suffered a similar fate had it and neighbouring buildings not been purchased by a heritage-loving architect named Paul Paget. Paget wished to restore the building for use as a home and as premises for his architectural company. The building's treasures include leaded windows bearing historical graffiti in the form of the signatures of distinguished visitors such as Queen Elizabeth the Queen Mother and Sir Winston Churchill (allegedly etched with a diamond pen).

Right: The Gatehouse of the Hospital of St. Bartholomew featuring London's only public statue of King Henry VIII

Sir John Betjeman, Britain's colourful Poet Laureate and architectural conservationist, famed as much for his popular television documentaries as for his poems, was so taken by Cloth Fair when he came to dine with Paget in 1954 that he promptly declared: "But of course I've got to live here!" Paget obliged and leased the upper floor of No. 43 to this legendary eccentric, the very definition of the English Fogey. Betjeman continued to live here for 20 years (apart from a temporary relocation to Rotherhithe for several months after his secretary accidentally set fire to the flat by failing to turn off a tape recorder!).

As delightful as Paget's neighbours were, the proximity of their homes created an unnatural level of intimacy. Observing that neighbours could see him carving his Sunday lunch, Paget once joked that he should lean out of the window and hand them a plate. He and his partner, Lord Mottistone, soon set about acquiring the buildings opposite and immediately blocked the principal offending window. Ever the aesthete, Paget avoided the ugliness of a boarded window by commissioning an artist to paint a *tromp l'oeil*. The painting was of "The Sailor's Return", the happy reunion of a sailor, freshly returned from his travels, embracing his family. Betjeman adored this *tromp l'oeil* and was amused to hear local tour guides mistakenly describe it as an ancient painting erected to avoid London's notorious 18th century window tax. The somewhat faded image may still be seen from the street.

No. 41–42 Cloth Fair EC1A 7JQ is a private residence that is not open to the public.
ʊ: Barbican

Above: Tromp l'oeil painting of The Sailor's Return in the window of No. 43 Cloth Fair

Left: No. 41–42 Cloth Fair, the oldest house in London

Handel and Hendrix
UNLIKELY NEIGHBOURS

The broad sweep of London's rich musical heritage is writ large on the walls of No. 23 and No. 25 Brook Street. Affixed to the walls of these neighbouring houses are two of London's famous heritage "Blue Plaques", each one commemorating a famous resident: Baroque composer George Frideric Handel at No. 25 and legendary American rock musician and songwriter Jimi Hendrix at No. 23.

Handel's House, now the excellent Handel House Museum, was the composer's home from 1723 until his death in 1759. Some of the wold's greatest music was composed there, including *Messiah*, *Zadok the Priest*, and *Music for the Royal Fireworks*.

Below: Blue Plaques on Nos. 23 & 25 Brook Street commemorating Handel and Hendrix

Right: The residence of Jimi Hendrix and the Handel House Museum

Above: Harpsichord in the main reception room at the Handel House Museum

In the 18th century foreigners were not permitted to own property in London and so when the German-born composer first arrived in London he was obliged to live with some of his wealthy patrons. Obtaining the sub-lease on Brook Street, his first private home, was a clear demonstration that Handel had achieved financial stability as well as professional and social success. The area around Brook Street was ideal for Handel: it was a respectable upper middle class neighbourhood and it was conveniently close to St. James's Palace, where Handel had been appointed "Composer of Musick for His Majesty's Chappel Royal", and The King's Theatre in the Haymarket, where his operas were performed.

After Handel's death the house passed through several owners, eventually undergoing conversion into a shop and office. The Handel House Trust, which had been set up to purchase the property and transform it into a museum, acquired the building in 2000 and opened it to the public in 2001.

Beautifully restored, the Handel House Museum provides the best possible insight into the lifestyle of this musical genius. Handel is believed to have performed informal concerts for friends in the main reception room (which housed his grandest harpsichord, a working replica of which is on display). Handel composed from an adjoining room and conducted business (such as selling musical scores and tickets) from the front parlour – could he possibly have imagined that 200 years later another iconic, but radically different, musician would be living in the house next door?

Arriving in London in 1966, Jimi Hendrix quickly became more famous in the UK than in his native America. His energy as a live performer and his willingness to play an intensive number of clubs across the city and the country, timed with the release of his critically-acclaimed albums, established Hendrix as an international music phenomenon. Following an American tour, Hendrix returned to London in 1968 and moved into a flat at No. 23 Brook Street, where he wrote songs, provided interviews, entertained guests and prepared for concerts. Upon discovering that Handel had lived next door, Hendrix immediately went to a nearby record shop to purchase Handel's *Messiah* and *Water Music*.

Like Handel, Hendrix found Brook Street's location ideal, not least because it was located a short walk from many of London's legendary music clubs and establishments. Hendrix only lived in the building for three months, but the connection was deemed sufficiently important to merit the installation of an official heritage blue plaque. The building is the only officially recognised Hendrix residence in the world. If walls could talk! Today the flat's rock and roll past is a distant memory and its current function is rather more mundane: it is currently used as the administrative offices of the Handel House Museum. Would Jimi approve?

Handel House Museum, 25 Brook Street, London, W1K 4HB
w: www.handelhouse.org
t: +44 (0)20 7495 1685
OPEN: Sun. closed; Tue–Wed 10am–6pm; Thu 10am–8pm; Fri–Sun 10am–6pm
U: Bond Street; Oxford Circus
ADMISSION: £

Above: Soho's Odd Couple: blue plaques on buildings either side of a restaurant commemorate two very different geniuses.

Handel and Hendrix aren't the only neighbourly odd couple to be found on London's streets. As commemorated in another pair of blue plaques, John Logie Baird, the inventor of television, first demonstrated his invention from a building two doors away from the house in which Wolfgang Amadeus Mozart lived and composed.

Sir John Soane's Museum
A HOUSE THAT DEFIES DESCRIPTION

If a house mirrors its owner, none has a clearer reflection than Sir John Soane's remarkable house at No. 12–14 Lincoln's Inn Fields. Every part of this building, from its exquisite contents to its ingenious design, is suffused with the character and memory of the great Georgian architect who built it and called it home. Brimming with delightful eccentricities, this bewitching house embodies some of the defining characteristics of the Enlightenment. Immortality may be unattainable but Sir John Soane lives on through his outstandingly original home.

King Seti's sarcophagus and *The Rake's Progress* by William Hogarth would be treasures in any location; but to find them squashed into an impossibly cluttered terraced house vying for attention with Graeco-Roman sculptures, English furniture, architectural fragments and thousands of other fascinating artefacts is thrillingly surreal. The imaginative use of architectural illusion, coloured glass, and hidden panels makes the heady atmosphere of the Soane Museum all the more potent.

One of Britain's most important and original architects, as famous for the buildings he designed but never built, as for those he did, Sir John Soane is best known for remodelling the Bank of England and for building Dulwich Picture Gallery, the first purpose-built public art gallery in Britain (and the inspiration for Britain's famous red telephone boxes). Alas, Soane's Bank of England was all but destroyed in the 1920s in an act described by one historian as "the greatest architectural crime in the City of London of the 20th century", leaving No. 12–14 Lincoln's Inn Fields, Dulwich Picture Gallery and Pitshanger Manor (Soane's country house in the modern London suburb of Ealing) as the only major examples of his work left in London. The rarity of Soane's work makes his house all the more special.

Soane acquired No. 12 Lincoln's Inn Fields in 1792, demolishing the existing 17th century house to build a new family home and offices for his architectural practice. Following his appointment as Professor of Architecture at the Royal Academy in 1806, Soane developed the idea of displaying his impressive collection of books, plaster casts, marbles and other artefacts so that his students might better access them. Soane eventually decided to purchase the neighbouring house and create a museum. Between 1808 and 1824 Soane acquired both No. 13 and No. 14, extending and combining them with No. 12 (although the front part of No. 14 was sold on as a private residence). In 1833 Soane successfully secured an Act of Parliament to preserve

Right: Sir John Soane's House and Museum

Left: Classical antiquities from Sir John Soane's collection

Below: The architectural adventure of a visit to Sir John Soane's House

the house and its contents for posterity. The Act came into force on his death in 1837 – ever since, the property has been maintained by a Curator and a board of trustees.

Walking past the grand terraces in leafy Lincoln's Inn Fields, visitors have no trouble identifying Soane's house – with its unusual projecting façade, Greek decorative pattern and statuary, it is hard to miss. The quirky tone of every visit is set from the start: visitors are required to ring the front door bell to gain entry, as if guests visiting a private home, but must then swiftly navigate past the enthusiastic staff members in the hallway before they can start exploring.

The clever use of light and the rich variety of style are amongst the greatest delights of the Soane Museum. The Breakfast Room's domed ceiling and convex mirrors have influenced architects across the globe, whilst the Pompeian red library/dining room conjures up thoughts of classical tombs. Walking through the cluttered basement to the great alabaster sarcophagus of Seti I that was unveiled here in 1825, it is difficult to imagine how 890 dignitaries were able to squeeze in to the house for the ceremony. Today, no more than 80 visitors are allowed in the building at any one time.

Sir John Soane's Museum, 13 Lincoln's Inn Fields, London, WC2A 3BP

w: www.soane.org
t: +44 (0)20 7405 2107
OPEN: Sun–Mon closed; Tue–Sat 10am–5pm
u: Holborn   **ADMISSION:** Free

Dennis Severs' House
LIVING HISTORY THROUGH SENSORY IMMERSION

To enter [Dennis Severs' House] is to pass through a frame into a painting, one with a time and a life of its own. DENNIS SEVERS' HOUSE WEBSITE

The air in Spitalfields hangs heavy with history. For three centuries this corner of old East London has been home to disparate groups of the world's dispossessed: Protestant Huguenots seeking sanctuary from religious persecution in France, the Irish escaping their national famine and Central European Jews fleeing anti-Semitic pogroms. By the late 19th century, this once respectable neighbourhood dominated by fine Georgian town houses had become London's most squalid slum, with one of its roads described as "perhaps the foulest and most dangerous street in the metropolis". These are the streets in which all five of Jack the Ripper's victims lived and in which, in 1888, two of them were murdered.

A hundred years after the Ripper murders, Spitalfields' older immigrant communities had been largely supplanted by Bangladeshi Muslims (nearby Brick Lane offers the best Balti outside the subcontinent) and its dilapidated Georgian town houses had been acquired by a passionate and varied group of artists, bohemians and Georgian architecture enthusiasts, who eagerly set about restoring them to their original glory. This group of pioneers initiated a process of gentrification that saw Spitalfields transform into one of the most desirable – and expensive – areas in the capital. One of the group's most imaginative and dedicated champions was Dennis Severs, a Californian artist who moved into a rundown Georgian terrace house in Folgate Street in 1979.

For the next twenty years, until his death in 1999, Severs used the ten rooms of his home as a canvas to create "still-life drama", devising interiors that the house might have had in the early 18th century, as the home of a Huguenot silk-weaving family. The attention to detail defies description. The eagle eyed will notice that one interior, featuring a knocked over chair and spilled bottles, is inspired by the bawdy scene depicted in a painting on the wall.

Above: Has the family just left?

Left: The elegant Georgian façade of Dennis Severs' House offers no clue to the delights that lie within

Above: Life imitating art at Dennis Severs' House: The scene is inspired by the painting on the wall

With its burning fire, distinct aromas and distant sounds, the atmosphere in the house suggests that the family is still in residence – the game is to move from room to room as if searching for them, all the time subtly progressing through almost two centuries of history. Many London houses are time capsules – only Dennis Severs' provides complete sensory immersion. Here Severs lived, by candlelight; a character in his own work of art. Dennis Severs described his house as "a collection of atmospheres: moods that harbour the light and spirit of various ages". The British artist David Hockney likened it to one of the world's greatest operas.

Severs bequeathed his home to The Spitalfields Trust and it is now open to the public. Visitors enter the house understanding that they are about to embark on a silent journey through time and life. To ensure the spell is not broken, speaking is discouraged and mobile phones must be switched off. A trip to Dennis Severs' House, we are told, "requires the same style of concentration as does an exhibition of Old Masters."

Dennis Severs' House, 18 Folgate Street, London, E1 6BX

W: www.dennissevershouse.co.uk
T: +44 (0)20 7247 4013
U: Shoreditch High Street; Liverpool Street
ADMISSION: £

Dennis Severs' House is only open on Sundays, selected Mondays and selected evenings. See website for further details.

No. 7 Hammersmith Terrace
ARTS & CRAFTS

Emery Walker was an English engraver, photographer and printer who played an active role at the centre of the English Arts & Crafts Movement, an international design movement that flourished between 1860 and 1910. His little-known 1750s house on the north bank of the River Thames preserves the only authentic Arts & Crafts urban interior in Britain. Preserved precisely as it was in Emery Walker's lifetime, the house has only recently been opened to the public and anyone interested in this unique and influential style of design is encouraged to visit.

Below: Dining Room at No. 7 Hammersmith Terrace

The Arts & Craft movement is best associated with Emery Walker's friend, the artist and designer William Morris, to whom Walker was an adviser. The Arts & Crafts movement was born out of concern for the impact of industrialisation on design and the traditional skills of the everyday labourer and craftsmen. The movement's emphasis on the quality and natural beauty of materials and the skill and art of the individual craftsman became extremely popular in the late 19th century, spreading across Europe and into North America.

No. 7 Hammersmith Terrace is a perfect example of a typical Arts & Crafts home. With wallpaper, furniture and textiles from Morris & Co., Middle Eastern and North African ceramics and 18th century furniture, the contents of the house are remarkably similar to those used by William Morris in his own home. Having lived at No. 3 Hammersmith Terrace for 25 years, Emery Walker moved to No. 7 in 1903, and remained there until his death in 1933. The house, with its preserved interior, was opened to the public by the Emery Walker Trust in 2005.

The property is open for pre-booked tours of no more than eight people. Visitors are shown the kitchen and the exquisitely decorated dining room, drawing room, back drawing room, bedroom and walled garden. Highlights include the only linoleum produced by William Morris that remains in its original domestic setting, letters from Rudyard Kipling and a teapot belonging to the pre-Raphaelite painter and figure, Dante Gabriel Rosetti.

7 Hammersmith Terrace, London, W6 9TS

w: www.emerywalker.org.uk
T: +44 (0)20 8748 2639
U: Stamford Brook
ADMISSION: £

The Emery Walker Trust conducts guided tours of 7 Hammersmith Terrace only on Saturdays and selected Sundays between April and October. See website for further details.

Right: Interior of the Octagon Room at Orleans House

Orleans House
A HIDDEN GEM

From Kensington Palace to Hampton Court, a narrow band of west and south west London contains the capital's greatest collection of royal and aristocratic country residences. Expertly restored and maintained properties such as Osterley Park, Chiswick, Boston Manor, Gunnersbury Park, Strawberry Hill and Pitshanger Manor remind us that, before the area was engulfed by monotonous suburban sprawl, it served as a peaceful and convenient country retreat. Fortunately, the great houses of west London, all now open to the public, retain enough surrounding parkland for visitors to appreciate how they appeared in their heyday, when they functioned as symbols and centres of power.

The greatest concentration of London's country houses is found close to the banks of a stretch of the River Thames that, whilst still firmly in London, is much more countryside than city. There are few more idyllic ways to spend a sunny afternoon in London than to stroll along the riverbank from the Royal Botanic Gardens at Kew to the funky enclave of artists' studios at Twickenham's Eel Pie Island. Far removed from any roads, cattle freely graze in riverside meadows. This serenely scenic route passes the opulent home of the Dukes of Northumberland (Syon Park and House), the smallest palace in Britain – if not all of Europe (Kew Palace), the ruins of a principal residence of the Tudor monarchs (old Richmond Palace), a stunning 18th century Palladian villa built for the mistress of King George II (Marble Hill House), one of the finest 17th century houses in Britain (Ham House), and finally the little known Orleans House.

Now tucked away in secluded gardens, Orleans House is a much overlooked Grade I listed Palladian villa that was constructed in 1710 for James Johnson, Secretary of State for Scotland. Johnson was a popular figure at court and King George I was one of the many great figures of the age entertained by him at his riverside villa. Visitors to the house were impressed by fine grounds that included a pleasure garden, a grotto, canals, an icehouse and wilderness. The house is named after the exiled French monarch, Louis, Duc d'Orleans, who lived there from 1813–1815. Louis would later reign as King Louis Philippe during France's so-called "July Monarchy" from 1830 to 1848.

By the 20th century Orleans House had become derelict and in 1926 much of it was demolished. Due in large part to the efforts of the wealthy Shell Oil heiress and art collector, the Hon. Nellie Ionides, nee Samuels (1883–1962), some parts survived, most notably the impressive baroque Octagon Room designed by James Gibbs, and the historic North Wing. The building now functions as the Orleans House Gallery and is home to the Richmond upon Thames Art Collection (much of which was donated by Ionides).

Orleans House is best visited as part of the aforementioned riverside walk, or in combination with a trip to nearby Marble Hill or Ham House. A delightfully unusual means of travel is available via Hammertons Ferry, a small motor boat "foot ferry" that carries pedestrians the short distance from Ham House on the south bank of the Thames to Marble Hill and Orleans House on the north bank. This service is the last privately-owned foot ferry on the Thames and adds to the area's unique and rarefied country character.

Orleans House Gallery, Riverside, Twickenham, TW1 3DJ

w: www.richmond.gov.uk/orleans_house_gallery
T: +44 (0)20 8831 6000
OPEN: Mon closed; Tue–Sat 1pm–4:30pm; Sunday & Bank Holidays 2pm–4:30pm (Oct–Mar); Tue–Sat 1pm–5:30pm; Sunday & Bank Holidays 2pm–4:30pm (Apr–Sep)
U: Richmond; Twickenham
ADMISSION: Free

Above: Octagon Room at Orleans House

CHAPTER FOUR

PUBS

The pub is an integral part of British culture and an intrinsic feature of the London streetscape, as familiar as the red pillar box or telephone box. For centuries, pubs, or "public houses", have been at the centre of local community life, providing a warm and welcoming space to socialise with friends and neighbours, catch up on local news, hold meetings and conduct business. They often functioned as an extension of the living room; an escape from drab and cramped homes. To this day, the image of the pub as the community linchpin is perpetuated in the most popular British soap operas, but this nostalgic picture is increasingly out of kilter with the reality of modern life.

Left: The well-worn interior of Gordon's Wine Bar

Changing habits, lifestyles and demographics are putting London's 7,000 pubs through their greatest test, with approximately five pubs shutting their doors for good every day. Situated on expensive prime real estate, many pubs are also sold to developers keen to convert them into luxury apartments.

Tough times have forced pubs to rise to the challenge and improve and expand their offerings. Shabby, smoke-filled boozers offering little more than warm beer and crisps have been transformed in to cutting-edge gastro pubs serving organic food and an extensive selection of premium beers and wines. This process of modernisation and gentrification has eliminated the old world charm (and often the old world characters) of many pubs but thankfully a large number retain their traditional neighbourhood feel.

Fortunately, due to their continuing appeal to both locals and tourists, the historic pubs of central London are in rude health. Many of these pubs are famed more for the famous customers than for their antiquity but it is often difficult to separate fact from fiction. If Dr. Samuel Johnson and Charles Dickens drank at every pub that has claimed their patronage, it is difficult to imagine they were ever sober enough to put pen to paper.

The Black Friar
A DRUNK MONK

London is home to several pubs of national historic significance however arguably only The Black Friar is a nationally significant work of art. Heavily influenced by Art Nouveau, The Black Friar's unique Arts & Crafts interior is a masterpiece of pub decoration, its extravagant design suitably playful for a palace of merrymaking. The pub and the surrounding area take their name from the 13th century Dominican priory that originally stood on the site, an association that dominates the pub's interior design. Housed in a small, four-storey triangular brick building almost as sharply angled as New York's famous Flatiron Building, the late 19th century pub stands on an urban island, hemmed in at the rear by the railway tracks leading to Blackfriars station.

On the pub's attractive exterior, the large statue of a beaming Black Friar provides the only clue to the visual feast that waits within. At first glance the interior's rich mosaics, marble and alabaster are more reminiscent of an Orthodox cathedral than a pub, but closer inspection of the brass reliefs that adorn the walls reveals a theme more Bacchanalian than Byzantine. A snoozing monk accompanied by the inscription "Industry is All" sums up the wit of the artist and architect responsible for creating this gem.

The turn of the century had seen a brief renaissance in investment in public houses, and The Black Friar's 1905 interior is one of the finest examples – the artistic detail and the quality of the materials is of the highest order. The pub is very popular with local workers and tourists, and seats in the marble recesses and alcoves are much sought after.

The survival of The Black Friar is in part due to the considerable effort of the late great architectural conservationist Sir John Betjeman. Like the dense collection of long-evaporated buildings that originally compressed it into its unusual shape, The Black Friar was once threatened with demolition; but with Grade II* listed heritage protection and a steady stream of patrons, its future seems very secure.

The Black Friar, 174 Queen Victoria Street, London, EC4V 4EG
w: www.nicholsonspubs.co.uk/theblackfriarblackfriarslondon
T: +44 (0)20 7236 5474
u: Blackfriars

Left: The richly decorated interior of The Black Friar

Above: The Cittie of Yorke

Left: The Black Friar

The Cittie of Yorke
WHERE SIZE MATTERS

Jaw-dropping is a term subject to overuse but it accurately describes the reaction of many first-time visitors to the Cittie of Yorke pub in Holborn. From the street the handsome Tudoresque pub has little to distinguish it from any of London's other period buildings; it is only upon walking through the long entrance passageway and emerging into the cavernous and wholly unexpected main bar that the pub's magnificence strikes the unsuspecting visitor into stunned silence.

Closer to a medieval great hall than a bar, the main room of the Cittie of Yorke is unique amongst London pubs. A soaring pitched roof supported by massive arched beams stands four storeys high, with a narrow and precarious looking walkway running just below. The bar is one of the longest in the country and is dominated by several immense 1000 gallon vats supported by impressive cast-iron columns. On the opposite side of the room, elegant wooden booths afford the discreet drinker privacy from prying eyes and pricked ears. Standing at the bar, perhaps with a tankard of ale, the traditional surroundings can easily conjure up feelings of nostalgia for Merrie Olde England and, indeed, this was the intention of the architect – for the Cittie of Yorke is not as old as it looks.

Although pubs have occupied the site since 1430, the current building is the result of an early 1920s redevelopment designed to hark back to a golden age of beer drinking. Some traces of previous incarnations remain, including the strange 19th century triangular fireplace that removes smoke via a flue under the floor. Now used as a subterranean bar, the brick cellars may date back to a coffee house that stood on the site in the 17th century.

Cittie of Yorke, 22 High Holborn, London, WC1V 6BN
T: +44 (0)20 7242 7670
U: Chancery Lane

Right: The cavernous great hall of the Cittie of Yorke

Dirty Dick's
A FILTHY TALE

This City pub on Bishopsgate by Liverpool Street station owes its unlikely name not to a lecherous old pirate or highwayman, as its name might suggest, but to a heartbroken 18th century dandy named Richard (or perhaps Nathaniel) Bentley. A successful ironmonger and warehouse owner, Bentley's world came crashing down when his fiancé died on their wedding day. Stricken with grief, so the legend goes, Bentley permanently locked the room in which the wedding feast was to be held and refused to wash or change his clothes ever again.

As Bentley lived out his remaining days in filth and squalour, surrounded by a growing number of dead cats, his reputation spread far and wide – letters sent to him were simply addressed to "The Dirty Warehouse, London". "Dirty Dick" Bentley's bizarre behaviour caused no harm to his business and upon his death in 1809 his story was capitalised on by the owners of the Old Jerusalem Tavern in Bishopsgate. Today, the tavern might be regarded as a pioneering "theme pub": it was renamed Dirty Dick's Old Port Wine & Spirit House and decorated with foul detritus, dust, cobwebs and dead cats.

Dirty Dick's legend grew steadily throughout the 19th century, with the pub even producing commemorative pamphlets about him. Charles Dickens was fascinated by this tale of a man who had sealed up the room of his wedding feast, and he is believed to have used Bentley as an inspiration for Miss Havisham in the novel *Great Expectations.*

Dirty Dick's was rebuilt in the 1870s, although the vaulted cellar – in which the restaurant is located – is of an earlier date. The dead cats and filthy contents of the legendary "Dustbin Bar" were cleared away in the 1980s and relegated to a rather more sanitary glass display case, where they may still be seen. Despite its sprucing up, the dimly lit pub, with its exposed timber and panelled rooms, retains much historic charm and is well worth a visit. Popular with City bankers, it would be nice to think that "dirty" martinis are a popular request!

Dirty Dick's, 202 Bishopsgate, London, EC2M 4NR
w: www.dirtydicks.co.uk
t: +44 (0)20 7283 5888
u: Bishopsgate

Left: Dirty Dick's   *Above:* The atmospheric interior of Dirty Dick's

Gordon's Wine Bar

With no shortage of historic venues in which to drink, Londoners can be quite blasé about their atmospheric surroundings; however a visit to Gordon's Wine Bar is bound to impress even the most worldly socialite. The bar's highlight, a dark, candle-lit cellar with blackened walls and an extremely low arched ceiling, is like nothing else in London. If the Phantom of the Opera opened a bar in London, it would probably look like Gordon's.

Opened in 1890, Gordon's is London's oldest wine bar, but its well-worn appearance makes it look even older. The perfectly preserved façade is a real gem, notable not for its beauty but for its rarity as an authentic Victorian bar front. Descending from street level via rickety steps, patrons entering the bar are struck first by its warmth and then by its shabbiness. Gordon's has turned dilapidation in to a design feature. The owners (a family coincidentally also named Gordon) have adopted a simple philosophy: don't ruin a successful formula. And so the bar is unchanged from 1890. Not only does this create a magical environment, it saves the considerable time and cost of refurbishment. The walls, tables and chairs are chipped and worn and the countless newspaper cuttings and memorabilia covering the walls have faded with age. The entire bar is coated in a brownish-yellow hue, the patina no doubt acquired through exposure to a century of tobacco and candle smoke.

The Villiers Street terrace in which Gordon's is located has a distinguished history. In the 1680s the great diarist Samuel Pepys lived on the site and Rudyard Kipling was a tenant in the building above from 1889–1891, perhaps becoming one of the bar's first patrons.

Gordon's is extremely popular with Londoners in the know and so, to fully appreciate the interior (and hopefully secure a seat), it is best visited on weekday afternoons, before the after work rush hour. On cold and rainy days, Gordon's provides the perfect bolt hole. Sitting in its warm subterranean chambers, steam rising from wet clothes, noisy chatter bouncing off the walls and the candlelight casting strange shadows, it is easy to imagine famous historical characters engaged in intrigue or plotting schemes from its darker corners. On sunny summer days, when the bar's warmth and lack of sunlight may not be as inviting, Gordon's opens its immense terrace on Watergate Walk, which runs along the south side of the bar. Until the construction of the Embankment in 1862, Watergate Walk would have been at the riverside.

Right: The cellar at Gordon's Wine Bar

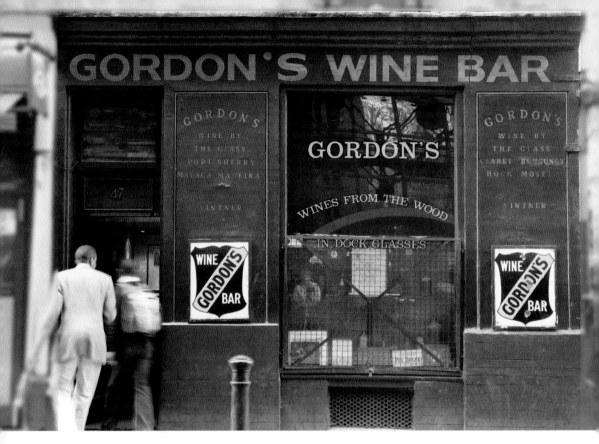

Above: The perfectly preserved façade of Gordon's Wine Bar

As its name suggests, Gordon's Wine Bar is not a pub – in fact, beer lovers should beware: only wines and fortified wines are served. But as one of London's most memorable drinking experiences this venerable wine bar certainly deserves a visit.

Gordon's Wine Bar, 47 Villiers Street, London, WC2N 6NE

w: www.gordonswinebar.com
т: +44 (0)20 7930 1408
u: Embankment

The Lamb & Flag
A BLOODY PAST

Now a smart, if slightly sterile, alley in slick Covent Garden, tiny Rose Street was once a haven for prostitutes and criminals, and it was here one night in December 1679 that the poet John Dryden was *"barbarously assaulted and wounded…by diverse men unknown"* as he made his way home from a local coffee house. The identity of Dryden's attackers remains a mystery but it is possible they were hired by the 2nd Earl of Rochester as a form of revenge for a bitingly satirical essay that Dryden was (mistakenly) thought to have written about the Earl and his mistress.

The assault may have lasted only a few minutes, but more than three centuries later the memory lingers in the historic Lamb & Flag pub and its Dryden Room. Watching the media types texting on their mobile phones in the bright cobbled courtyard outside the pub, it is difficult to imagine that 19th century thugs and bruisers once congregated in the same spot to participate in the vicious bare knuckle fights that earned the Lamb & Flag the nickname of "the Bucket of Blood".

Right: The Lamb & Flag

Originally called the Cooper's Arms, the pub was renamed the Lamb & Flag in the early 19th century. The image of the Lamb & Flag is the traditional Christian representation of Christ (the victorious Lamb of God – *Agnus Dei*) and it is found elsewhere in London, most famously as the symbol of Middle Temple.

The pub's brick façade dates from the 19th century but its interiors are much older – and the traditional features one would expect in an 18th century pub are here in great abundance. Approached via the historic covered passageway on the pub's right-hand side, it is reassuring to know that these timeless corners survive even in the centre of London's dynamic and ever-evolving West End.

The Lamb & Flag, 33 Rose Street, London, WC2E 9EB
w: www.lambandflagcoventgarden.co.uk
t: +44 (0)20 7497 9504
u: Leicester Square; Covent Garden

The Olde Wine Shades
LONDON'S OLDEST PUB

"Mirror, mirror on the wall, which is the oldest tavern of them all?" Claiming to be the oldest pub in London is good for business – and at least a dozen pubs currently vie for the title; however with tour guides, books and websites championing different candidates, often backed up with compelling arguments, identifying the oldest is no easy task. The issue is complicated because most ancient taverns have been frequently rebuilt – a pub with a five-hundred year history may have premises that are no more than two hundred years old.

Below: The Olde Wine Shades

If a pub's antiquity is determined by the length of time it has traded from its current building, rather than the length of time it has been trading from its current site, almost all of London's venerable taverns can be discounted, since many public houses were rebuilt after the Great Fire of London or during Georgian and Victorian redevelopment. Similarly, although The Hoop & Grapes at 47 Aldgate Street can rightly claim to occupy the oldest building of any pub in London, the late 16th century house was only converted into a pub in the 1890s. This leaves only two contenders for the title of "London's oldest pub": The Seven Stars (built in 1602) on Carey Street behind the Royal Courts of Justice and The Olde Wine Shades (built in 1663) on Martin Lane in the City.

Of these two pre-Great Fire survivors, only The Olde Wine Shades has been continuously licensed for more than 350 years, and so it seems fair to call it London's oldest pub. Sort of. For The Olde Wine Shades is now a wine bar under the ownership of the distinguished London wine merchant, El Vino – and so perhaps it would be more accurate to describe the venue as "London's oldest licensed establishment". Either way, in a city that delights in eccentricity it is a curious fact that London's oldest pub doesn't serve beer!

Located near the starting spot of the Great Fire of London, the survival of The Olde Wine Shades is miraculous. The pub itself is dark and atmospheric, although it has undergone minor modernisation, including the creation of a restaurant in the ancient cellars. A notable feature of the pub is the bricked-up entrance to a tunnel through which smugglers could evade duty by silently rowing their cargo up the river by night. The tunnel was accessible until sealed following a bombing raid in 1940, but in 2002 nearby construction work revealed the remains of a smuggler's skeleton.

The Olde Wine Shades, 6 Martin Lane, Cannon Street, London, EC4R 0DP

w: www.elvino.co.uk
T: +44 (0)20 7626 6876
u: Monument

The Sherlock Holmes

aker Street may be the area best associated with Sherlock Holmes but the world's greatest detective did not confine himself to that narrow part of town. Holmes' creator, Sir Arthur Conan Doyle, featured many London locations in his *Strand Magazine* mysteries, including Charing Cross station and nearby Northumberland Street; and it is on Northumberland Street that The Sherlock Holmes pub now stands – a major site of pilgrimage for fans of the enigmatic sleuth.

Below: Recreation of Sherlock Holmes' drawing room in The Sherlock Holmes pub

Previously known as the Northumberland Arms, this traditional London pub has no direct association with Sherlock Holmes but it is located either on or close to the site of the "Northumberland Hotel", the hotel in which Sir Henry Baskerville stayed on his arrival from Canada in *The Hound of the Baskervilles*. The pub is also situated near famous Old Scotland Yard and across from Craven Passage, location of the Turkish baths used by Holmes and Dr. Watson in *The Illustrious Client*.

The Sherlock Holmes pub contains the oldest and most important collection of Sherlock Holmes' memorabilia ever assembled, large enough to merit classification as a small museum. Brought together for the 1951 Festival of Britain, the collection was purchased by hospitality company Whitbread & Co. in 1957 to form the basis of the Holmes-themed pub that survives today.

The exhibits have not been moved since they were first installed, and include a service revolver that Dr. Watson might have used, illustrations from the *Strand Magazine* and the mounted head of the dreaded hound of the Baskervilles. A muted and non-intrusive television in one corner of the room plays television adaptations of the Sherlock Holmes mysteries. The jewel in the pub's crown, however, is undoubtedly the meticulous recreation of Holmes' cluttered drawing room. Located by the entrance to the upstairs restaurant, the furnished room contains Holmes' violin, morphine syringes, chemistry equipment, and various artefacts associated with his many escapades. By the window is the bullet-holed mannequin of Holmes which the detective used to foil his assassination in *The Empty House*.

The Sherlock Holmes, 10–11 Northumberland Street, Craven Passage, London, WC2N 5DB

w: www.sherlockholmespub.com
T: +44 (0)20 7930 2644
U: Charing Cross; Embankment

The Ten Bells
JACK THE RIPPER'S LOCAL?

Modern Spitalfields is a hipster hangout, a haven for hedge fund managers and a home for world-famous artists such as Tracey Emin and Gilbert & George. Yet as recently as the 1980s it was a derelict and decaying backwater, an embarrassing eyesore on the edge of the affluent City. Since then, a sensitive grassroots gentrification has seen the restoration of Spitalfields' fine Georgian houses and the regeneration of its commercial life. Such revitalisation has profoundly changed the character of the area yet in the midst of this remarkable

Below: The Ten Bells

Above: No longer a slum. Fournier Street, with Christ Church and the Ten Bells at the far end, is now an exclusive London address.

renewal one establishment, The Ten Bells, has remained a constant, anchoring Spitalfields to its weighty past.

Standing in the shadow of Nicholas Hawksmoor's slightly sinister Christ Church, The Ten Bells has been a companion of the 18th century religious masterpiece for all but 25 years. The proximity of pub and pulpit has even influenced the tavern's name, which was first known as the Eight Bells Alehouse in 1755, only becoming The Ten Bells after Christ Church increased its peal of bells from eight to ten in 1788. The pub originally stood several metres from its current location on the corner of Fournier Street and Commercial Street, the earlier building having been demolished in 1851 as part of a road-widening scheme.

In the latter half of the 19th century Spitalfields was one of London's most notorious slums.

By this time, the skilled French Huguenot silk workers who had settled there in the 18th century were a distant memory, supplanted by Jewish and Eastern European refugees, their fine Georgian houses abandoned to London's most downtrodden and wretched.

It was in this cholera-stricken neighbourhood near Whitechapel that five of Jack the Ripper's victims lived. Two of them, the prostitutes Annie Chapman and Mary Jane Kelly, are known to have frequented The Ten Bells and it is thought that Chapman may have had a drink there on the night of her murder. The Ripper himself may have propped up the bar at some point during his rampage of 1888.

The Whitechapel Murders alerted wider society to the squalour of the worst slums of East London and this resulted in the demolition of many of the sites connected with the victims. The Ten Bells is a rare survivor and one of the most important sites associated with the story of Jack the Ripper. Not surprisingly, the pub is a popular stopping point for Ripper walking tours and it regularly features in books and on screen, including in the film *From Hell*, in which the actor Johnny Depp (playing a Scotland Yard investigator) is filmed having a drink with Mary Jane Kelly. Between 1976 and 1988 the pub was renamed "The Jack the Ripper" and filled with Ripper memorabilia; however it reverted to its previous name on the centenary of the murders, partly out of respect for the victims.

Today the Grade II listed heritage building caters for a trendy clientele and this is reflected in the furnishings, but the walls have been perfectly preserved and feature some beautiful Victorian tiling, including a late 19th century mural of old Spitalfields. A 21st century mural reflecting new Spitalfields depicts the areas contemporary characters and scenes.

The Ten Bells, 84 Commercial Street, London, E1 6LY

w: www.tenbells.com
t: +44 (0)7530 492986
u: Aldgate East; Liverpool Street

Ye Olde Cheshire Cheese
A FLEET STREET FRISSON

Perhaps London's most famous historic pub, Ye Olde Cheshire Cheese is not an obvious choice for inclusion in a book about the capital's lesser-known sights. With its delightfully complicated warren of small, dimly lit rooms, some set out much as they were in the 18th century, the Cheshire Cheese frequently tops lists of the best pubs in the City, and it is one of the few to be visited by as many tourists as locals. However, amongst all the grand tales of merrymaking by Charles Dickens, Samuel Johnson and the many other witty luminaries who frequented the pub following its reconstruction in 1667, there is a seedier – but no less interesting – history which is seldom mentioned.

In 1962 a serious fire on the upper level of the Cheshire Cheese revealed amongst the debris a series of highly explicit erotic relief tiles depicting figures engaged in all manner of creative sexual activity. The tiles are too lewd to be reproduced in this book, but some of the more memorable scenes include a woman spanking a man with a bundle of twigs and a woman using a rope to lower herself in a basket onto an excited man waiting below. Thankfully, a few of the characters in the tiles were thoughtful enough to keep some of their clothes on, and this has enabled art historians to date the titles to the mid to late 18th century.

Brothels and men's drinking clubs were all the rage in the 18th century and given the upstairs location in which the tiles were found, it is reasonable to assume that at least one room in the Cheshire Cheese was used for bawdy sessions. The tiles were not expensive to produce and were fairly common at the time, though the ones at the Cheshire Cheese are remarkably rare survivors. Many experts believe the tiles would have been kept out of sight during the day, only to be hung up when the upstairs room was available for ribald activity. The blackened appearance of many of the tiles suggests they were placed near the fireplace, the flames of which would have illuminated the figures in all their glory.

The tiles were given to the Museum of London soon after their discovery but were deemed too explicit for the eyes of the public, remaining hidden from sight until briefly brought out on public display in February 2014 for "City and Seduction", an adult's only late night exhibition to mark Valentine's Day.

The Cheshire Cheese tiles are part of London's long and lustful sexual history, a 2,000-year

Right: Ye Olde Cheshire Cheese, rebuilt 1667

Above: The vaulted cellars of Ye Olde Cheshire Cheese

narrative that includes Roman bathhouses, medieval bawdy houses and Victorian fleshpots. With so many London exhibits devoted to murder, torture and horror, one would hope that society is mature enough for these cheeky tiles to be put on permanent display, and perhaps even for copies to be installed in the original room at the Cheshire Cheese (where they would be sure to create a stir!).

Ye Olde Cheshire Cheese is a Grade II listed heritage building and its nationally significant interior has been written about extensively. Although the original pub of 1538 was destroyed by fire, the impressive vaulted cellars were probably part of a 13th century Carmelite monastery that once stood on the site.

Ye Olde Cheshire Cheese, 145 Fleet Street, London, EC4A 2BU
T: +44 (0)20 7353 6170
U: Blackfriars

Right: Ye Old Mitre

Ye Olde Mitre
THE FASTEST WAY TO LEAVE LONDON

Ye Olde Mitre is a difficult place to find. Hidden in a tiny courtyard that is accessed via a narrow alleyway marked only by an old street lamp bearing a small sign in the shape of a bishop's mitre, it is no surprise that staff in the nearby diamond shops of Hatton Garden have never heard of Ye Old Mitre. To further complicate matters, this central London pub isn't even in London – it's in Cambridgeshire! Yes. Cambridgeshire. But those who persevere in their quest to locate this ancient tavern will find it a rewarding experience.

Ye Olde Mitre's curious Cambridgeshire connection rests upon its centuries-old association with the Bishops of Ely, from whose headgear the pub's name derives. Located in Ely Court,

Above: The cosy snug in Ye Olde Mitre

just off of Ely Place, the pub was built on lands that constituted the Cambridgeshire bishops' London seat. Today 13th century St. Etheldreda's Church, the oldest surviving Catholic Church in England, is all that remains of the Bishops' palace.

Ely Place remains London's last privately owned ancient road, as evidenced by the grand gates, security barriers and guard lodge at its intersection with Charterhouse Street – and when Ely Place was shut nightly at 10pm, so was Ye Old Mitre. Until relatively recently, top-hatted beadles hired by the Commissioners of Ely (the land's governing body) would have patrolled the vicinity as it was beyond the jurisdiction of the City of London police. The belief that London's police were only allowed entrance to Ely Place by invitation of the Commissioners led thieves to advise their partners in crime to run through the area if trying to escape capture by pursuing "Bobbies".

Ely Place's curious status led to a London riddle: standing in the centre of the City, what is the fastest way to leave London? The answer of course was to have a drink at Ye Olde Mitre.

Ye Olde Mitre was originally constructed in 1547 to serve the servants of the Palace of the Bishops of Ely but the current pub was not built until 1772. The handsome timber-fronted building stands in the tiny courtyard as if an island, a stone mitre from the demolished palace's gatehouse embedded in its front wall. The charming interior was remodelled in the 1930s but retains some fascinating features, most notably a cherry tree incorporated in to the corner of the front bar. In the 1570s Sir Christopher Hatton had leased much of the surrounding land from the Bishops of Ely and the cherry tree is said to have marked the boundary between the Bishop's land and that of Hatton. Legend attests that Queen Elizabeth I and Sir Christopher once danced a pretty jig around this tree as if it were a maypole. Ye Olde Mitre may no longer obtain its operating licence from Cambridgeshire, but its territorial status remains one of London's oddest anomalies.

Ye Olde Mitre, 1 Ely Place, London, EC1N 6SJ

w: www.yeoldemitreholborn.co.uk
T: +44 (0)20 7405 4751
U: Chancery Lane

THE CORNHILL THREE

Fuelled by Victorian pulp fiction and 20th century Hollywood, the London of popular imagination is a warren of dimly-lit narrow lanes closed in with top heavy buildings and thick fog. The city of Sherlock Holmes, Oliver Twist and Jack the Ripper was once as much fact as fiction but today "a foggy day in old London town" is a very rare thing, and only pockets of London's latticework of lanes retain their historic atmosphere.

After Fleet Street and the Strand, London's greatest concentration of old-fashioned alleys is to be found around the thoroughfare of Cornhill, a City artery with a capillary network of fourteen alleys and courtyards. This maze once bustled with activity as strolling window shoppers frustrated the impatient workers who used its alleys as a shortcut. The densely packed homes, shops and businesses ensured a steady flow of custom for the many coffee houses that began to appear around Cornhill in the 18th century, in large part because of the proximity of the Royal Exchange. Deemed too vulgar to enter the Exchange, stockbrokers had little option but to engage in share and commodity trading from the lively coffee houses on and around Exchange Alley (now Change Alley). The coffee houses of Cornhill were the forerunners of the London Stock Exchange (which was founded here in long-vanished Sweeting's Alley) and the name of one, Lloyd's Coffee House, survives today in the specialist insurance market known as *Lloyd's of London*. Lloyd's Coffee House was situated on Pope's Head Alley, an alley that, like nearby Castle Court and Sun Court, took its name from its most notable tavern.

Right: St. Michael's Alley, Cornhill

Above: The Jamaica Wine House

It was in this characterful labyrinth that Charles Dickens placed the counting house of Ebenezer Scrooge, the cold-hearted miser who found redemption on Christmas Eve. Perhaps no novel is more evocative of the spirit of 19th century London than *A Christmas Carol*, and no part of London is more evocative of the spirit of *A Christmas Carol* than Cornhill. Scuttling through the alleys in a winter blizzard, it is easy to imagine that at any moment one might bump into Scrooge's fun-loving assistant Bob Cratchitt, perhaps once again hurrying to go "down a slide on Cornhill, at the end of a lane of boys" while making his way home to Camden.

The precise spot of Scrooge's counting house is unknown but in *A Christmas Carol* Dickens writes that it was situated in a courtyard facing "the ancient tower of a church, whose gruffold bell was always peeping down at Scrooge out of a Gothic window in the wall." The tower is likely to be the famed tower of the Church of St. Michael-in-Cornhill, which could place Scrooge's counting house across the street from the church, in tiny Newman's Court. When Scrooge left his counting house to take "his usual melancholy dinner in his usual

Right: The George & Vulture

melancholy tavern", it is possible that he went to one of three historic hostelries which were well known to Charles Dickens and which still offer hearty fare to local workers today.

Running along the west wall of St. Michael-in-Cornhill, pretty St. Michael's Alley is home to the Jamaica Wine House, an attractive but unusual pub with a fascinating history. As indicated by the ceramic plaque embedded in the outside wall, the Jamaica Wine House (better known to locals as "the Jampot") stands on the site of London's first coffee house: "at the sign of Pasqua Rosee's Head" (also known as "The Turk's Head"). The coffee house was opened in 1652 by the English merchant Daniel Edwards (who *brought* the coffee beans) and his Greek manservant Pasqua Rosee (who *brewed* the coffee beans), and offered Londoners a revolutionary sensory and social experience. The famous diarist Samuel Pepys visited in 1660 and wrote "the first time that ever I was there, and I found much pleasure in it." The current pub, with its unique red stone walls and classic Victorian features, dates from 1869 and is a Grade II listed heritage building.

Passing the Jamaica Wine House, a right turn into picture perfect Castle Court leads to the George & Vulture, an inn with an impeccable Dickensian pedigree. Built in 1748, the George & Vulture is an authentic London chophouse so firmly established as a City institution that,

despite being hard to find, it has no need for a website and no need to open outside weekday lunchtime. Such confidence is understandable considering that an inn has stood on this site since at least the 15th century, and possibly earlier.

The original inn, then known only as the "George", was destroyed in the Great Fire of London in 1666. When the tavern was rebuilt, the landlord of the George agreed to rent part of the building to a neighbouring wine merchant whose own property had also succumbed to the flames. The wine merchant's sign of business was a live vulture which, unsurprisingly, concerned the landlord of the George. Worried by the unsettling effect the bird was having on customers, the landlord and the wine merchant settled on a compromise and the name of the tavern was changed to the George & Vulture.

Entering the George & Vulture is to walk into the pages of a Dickens novel – and indeed the George & Vulture is world renowned for its numerous appearances in *The Pickwick Papers,* where it served as Mr. Pickwick's London residence. Charles Dickens was fond of the venue and is known to have dined and stayed there – to this day, the great man's bust and other memorabilia are notable features in the restaurant. So strong is the association with Charles Dickens that the City Pickwick Club and Dickens Pickwick Club both use the George & Vulture for functions, and his descendants have held their Christmas lunch in the "Dickens' Room".

Below: Interior of the George & Vulture   *Right:* Simpsons Tavern

Unsurprisingly, the George & Vulture is reputed to have had many other famous patrons, not least Jonathan Swift, the author of *Gulliver's Travels*, and Daniel Defoe, the creator of Robinson Crusoe.

The George & Vulture continues to serve the same hearty fare that would have been enjoyed by the Victorians and Georgians: roast beef, sausages, steak and kidney pie. The service is wonderfully old fashioned, with the staff finely tuned to the needs of their long-standing City customers. The perfectly preserved Grade II listed heritage interior would be instantly recognisable to Dickens and, as tourists rarely venture in to the George & Vulture, a meal at this insider's institution truly feels like an authentic London experience.

From the George & Vulture taking a sharp right turn into narrow Ball Court, leads directly to Simpson's Tavern, the City's other ancient chop house. Not to be confused with the larger (and slightly younger) Simpson's in the Strand, Simpson's Tavern has been serving satisfying hot meals from this tiny courtyard location since 1757. The Tavern was established by London restaurateur

Above: Lunchtime in the grill room at Simpson's Tavern

Thomas Simpson on land he received from his father – and the menu and layout has barely changed since.

Simpson's is spread over three floors of what were once two traditional City houses. The principal feature of the fine wood panelled entranceway is an attractive bay window that affords a tantalising glimpse of the famed grill room. Seating in the grill room is arranged in stalls that can accommodate up to six customers each. This layout would have been familiar to any Victorian gentleman, as evidenced by the 19th century brass rails above each stall that were used for the safekeeping of top hats. If Simpson's has a masculine feel, this will be because women were not admitted until 1916, although Simpson's was an early employer of women. The staff at Simpson's are a vital part of its appeal, and the tavern is one of the few City employers where it is possible to have a job for life.

Simpson's is an institution that celebrates its heritage without standing on ceremony. The napkins are paper, the butter is foil wrapped and the table cloths are non-existent. This is a tavern that provides good traditional fare with an honest, no-nonsense attitude. Simple, reliable and welcoming, Simpson's recipe for success is no secret and should keep customers satisfied for another 250 years.

Overleaf: The Ministry of Defence Main Building houses Henry VIII's Wine Cellar, a remnant of the Palace of Whitehall which was destroyed by fire in 1698

CHAPTER FIVE

BUILDINGS

London is a city of constant renewal and evolution. Cranes permanently clutter the London skyline, even during the deepest recessions.

The square mile of the City of London, the ancient heart of the metropolis, is filled with shimmering skyscrapers – 21st century giants squeezed into medieval streets, their foundations resting upon Roman remains.

Development is the battle cry of a competitive mercantile city but, for historic cities such as London, it has often been achieved at the expense of heritage. The destruction meted out to the city by 19th and 20th century developers and urban planners in the name of progress was no less devastating than the Great Fire of 1666 and the Blitz of 1940–1941. Almost as many books can be written about the buildings London lost as about those that remain.

It was the 1960s demolition of the Euston Arch – the stunning early Victorian gateway to Euston Railway Station – that finally awoke Londoners to the plight of their historic buildings. Since then, London has had an active conservation movement which has gradually elevated heritage to the status of a civic religion, with the city's historic buildings now venerated as sacrosanct.

This newfound passion ("the zeal of the converted") is not restricted to the preservation of London's grandest and most celebrated buildings but also includes those smaller, but no less worthy, structures that stand in their shadows. Throughout London, an extraordinary range of buildings, the hotchpotch footprints of those who came before, stand as markers in historically unrecognisable terrain – they are legacies left to London, some more famous than others, but all possessing secret histories and curious tales that deserve to be told.

All Hallows by the Tower
A LONDON PECULIAR

All Hallows by the Tower represents the very best of peculiar London: a modern institution that is also an ancient relic, a giant curiosity cabinet, and a bit player in history. Founded in 675AD, the church is impressively old, predating the neighbouring Tower of London by more than three centuries, but as a site of habitation it is even older. The church stands on the site of a Roman house constructed in the late 2nd century, built at about the same time as the nearby Roman wall, part of which still stands by Tower Hill station. Remarkably, down in the church crypt, a well-preserved section of the house's Roman pavement – one of the finest in London – may be seen in its original position.

All Hallows by the Tower claims to be the oldest church in London and, while this cannot be proved beyond doubt, there is little reason to quibble. Despite extensive rebuilding over the course of its history, it took a bomb blast in 1940 to reveal that a wall in the west nave retains an original Saxon arch. The arch is believed to be the oldest surviving piece of extant church fabric in London and is one of a number of Saxon artefacts that may be seen on display.

The church's proximity to the Tower Hill scaffold made it an obvious temporary resting place for many of the individuals who were beheaded at that bloody spot. Some of the Catholic martyrs of the English Reformation, such as Saint John Fisher (d. 1535) and Saint Thomas More (d. 1535), had their bodies unceremoniously thrown into the churchyard of All Hallows, often remaining there for days or weeks, before their remains were transported elsewhere for burial. Following his execution in 1645, William Laud, former Archbishop of Canterbury, lay in All Hallows for twenty years before his body was removed to St. John's College Oxford.

Above: All Hallows by the Tower

Left: Roman pavement c.200AD in the crypt of All Hallows by the Tower

Samuel Pepys famously climbed the tower of All Hallows to watch the early stages of the Great Fire of 1666, only leaving when it was feared that the church might also be consumed. But it is in the crypt, rather than the tower, that the church's greatest treasures are to be found. Housed in the Saxon section of the church, the delightfully quirky crypt museum holds an impressive number of historically significant artefacts, including the church registers that record the baptism of William Penn, the founder of Pennsylvania, and the marriage of John Quincy Adams, the sixth president of the United States of America. The most unexpected item is the barrel that was used as a crow's nest on *The Quest*, the ship in which the polar explorer Sir Ernest Shackleton died in 1922 during his final voyage to the Antarctic. All Hallows by the Tower is a true London peculiar.

All Hallows by the Tower, Byward Street, London, EC3R 5BJ

w: www.allhallowsbythetower.org.uk
T: +44 (0)20 7481 2928
OPEN: Check with the church for opening times
U: Tower Hill

Above: Crow's nest from *The Quest*, the ship in which Sir Ernest Shackleton died during his final voyage to the Antarctic

Right: Baker Street station: the world's oldest and best-preserved underground platform

Baker Street Station
THE WORLD'S OLDEST SUBWAY SYSTEM

Loved and loathed in equal measure, London's underground system is the beating heart of the city, pumping millions of people around the metropolis every day. "The Tube" is often taken for granted but without it London's arteries would clog up and the city would stop. Until recently, London had the world's longest subway system, with New York snapping close at its heels; however, extraordinarily rapid infrastructure development in Seoul, Shanghai and Beijing has now pushed London into fourth place. London's subway system may no longer be the world's longest or busiest, but it will always retain one title: the world's oldest.

London opened the first underground railway on 10 January 1863, decades before its nearest rivals in Paris (1900), Berlin (1902) and New York (1902). The idea was radical and many commentators were appalled at the notion that people might wish to travel in such a "sordid" and "inhuman" manner. As *The Times* reported, it was an: "insult to common sense…to suppose that people…would ever prefer…to be driven amid palpable darkness through the foul subsoil of London … as a merely quicker medium [to the bus]."

Known as the Metropolitan Railway (from which the name of the Parisian "*Métropolitain*"

derives), the system originally used steam locomotives to transport passengers under the streets of London. To counter any health concerns, corporate bosses even claimed that the steam-filled platforms provided a form of "health resort" for asthma sufferers – meanwhile, staff were permitted to grow beards to act as a filter against the vapours. By the end of the century, steam locomotives had had their day as a means of underground travel and in 1890 the Metropolitan Railway became the world's first electrified railway system.

The Metropolitan Railway's first line stretched from Paddington to Farringdon, connecting the major railway termini of Paddington, Euston, King's Cross and St. Pancras. Baker Street is

Above: An old platform sign at Baker Street station directs commuters to "Metroland", a section of north west suburban London that developed due to the proximity of the Metropolitan line

one of the seven original stations opened on the line and the original platform, now used by the Hammersmith & City line, looks almost exactly as it did in 1863. Descriptive panels on the platform walls provide further historical information and illustrations.

Standing on the spacious platform, beneath its grand sweeping arch, it is not difficult to imagine the first locomotives emerging from the tunnels, filling the station with billowing clouds of steam. In January 2013, to mark the 150th anniversary of the London Underground, crowds of people filled Baker Street and the other historic station platforms to see an original steam locomotive once again travel the original route.

Baker Street station, Marylebone Road, London, NW1 5LA

w: www.tfl.gov.uk

u: Baker Street

Brick Lane Mosque
CHANGING FAITH

No building in the United Kingdom represents the evolution of immigration patterns better than the Brick Lane Mosque on the corner of Fournier Street in East London's Spitalfields. It is one of the few buildings in the world (if there are any others) to have functioned as a church, a synagogue and a mosque.

Built in 1743 as a chapel to serve the French protestant Huguenot community that had settled in Spitalfields after fleeing persecution in their native Catholic France, the chapel even-

tually became Weslyan (1809) and then Methodist (1819). By the middle of the 19th century Jewish immigrants fleeing programs in Russia had settled in East London in large numbers and in 1897 the chapel building was converted into the Spitalfields Great Synagogue.

The synagogue remained in use until the 1960s, by which time, like the Huguenots before them, most of the Jewish population had left the area for more affluent parts of the city. Since the 1960s, the newest and largest wave of immigration has been from the subcontinent, primarily Muslims from India and Bangladesh. In 1976, the now closed synagogue was opened as the Brick Lane Mosque and it has served the Muslim community ever since.

At the top of the building's main façade, an 18th century sundial with a Latin inscription by a pagan philosopher is an incongruous and unexpected element to find on a mosque. The inscription, by Horace, is UMBRA SUMUS ("We Are Shadows") – in the context of the building's history it could not be more appropriate.

Brick Lane Mosque, 59 Brick Lane, London, E1 6QL
w: www.bricklanejammemasjid.co.uk
T: +44 (0)20 7841 3600
OPEN: The Mosque is a place of worship and is not open to the public.
u: Aldgate East; Whitechapel

Above: Façade featuring the original 1743 sundial bearing an inscription by Horace: UMBRA SUMUS – "We Are Shadows"

Left: Local community centre and Brick Lane Mosque (far right)

Brompton Oratory
KGB DEAD LETTER BOX

Brompton Oratory, the ornate, highly Italianate and ultra-traditional Roman Catholic Church in exclusive Knightsbridge is not a place one would normally associate with the godless Soviet Union. But during the Cold War, KGB secret agents identified this darkly lit church as the safest place in London for use as a "Dead Letter Box", a place where microfilm and small packages could be left for collection.

As late as 1985, Soviet agents issued instructions stating that the Oratory's dead letter box was located behind two pillars standing immediately to the left of a copy of Michelangelo's statue "Pieta", which is located just inside the entrance to the church, on the right-hand side. In the 1990s a former spy reported that once an agent had deposited an item in the church he was expected to travel to Mayfair to leave a discreet chalk mark on the lamppost that still stands in tiny Audley Square.

The KGB seem to have been extraordinarily keen on Knightsbridge because they identified a second location for a dead letter box immediately behind the Brompton Oratory in the grounds of Holy Trinity Church. Running along the east side of the Oratory, Cottage Place is a narrow alley that connects Holy Trinity to the Brompton Road. An agent walking up Cottage Place would soon come upon a small walled area containing a tree and a statue of St. Francis of Assisi. The dead letter box was located in the space between the tree and the wall.

How frequently these dead letter boxes were used is unknown and at least one agent believed them to be risky. Still, it is remarkable to think that during the height of the Cold War, as parishioners of the Brompton Oratory prayed for friends and family trapped behind the Iron Curtain, a few feet away Soviet agents may have been engaged in espionage.

The area's Cold War connections do not end with these two dead letter boxes. Many people visiting the Brompton Oratory leave the area via nearby South Kensington station, often stopping off at Daquise, the legendary Polish café and restaurant that has been operating next to the station since 1947. Popular with secret agents throughout the Cold War, this unassuming old-world establishment is best known for its role in the Profumo Affair, the scandal that almost brought down the British Government in the 1960s. The Profumo Affair erupted following the revelation that John Profumo, the British Secretary of State for War, had been involved in an illicit affair with London call girl Christine Keeler, a lover of Yevgeni Ivanov, naval attaché of the Soviet Embassy and KGB spy. Ivanov and Keeler were regular customers at Daquise and it is thought that one of the purposes of their meetings was for Keeler to pass on the information she was able to extract from Profumo during their secret encounters.

The London (Brompton) Oratory, Brompton Road, London, SW7 2RP

W: www.bromptonoratory.com
T: +44 (0)20 7808 0900
OPEN: Mon–Sun 6am–8pm
U: Knightsbridge; South Kensington

Above: Site of a KGB Dead Letter Box on the grounds of Holy Trinity Church, Brompton

Left: The Church of the Immaculate Heart of Mary, better known as Brompton Oratory

The College of Arms
GARTERS & DRAGONS

The British adore pageantry and their reputation for flawless state ceremonial is world-renowned. Much of the credit for this meticulous attention to detail is due in part to the expertise of the heralds of The College of Arms, the official body in charge of heraldry, flags, precedence and major state occasions such as coronations and state funerals.

The heralds hold even more exotic titles, including "Bluemantle", "Rouge Croix", "Clarenceux" and "Lancaster". Correct form dictates that heralds should be addressed by their historic title rather than by their Christian name or surname. There can be no doubt that a meeting with "Garter King of Arms", "Rouge Dragon" or "Portcullis" sounds a lot more interesting than a meeting with "Mr. Jones", "Mr. Smith" or "Mr. Brown".

Below: The College of Arms is a living piece of medieval England in 21st century London. Founded in 1484, it researches and registers family trees, designs and grants coats of arms, and advises on matters relating to noble titles. The College's thirteen heralds in ordinary are correctly known as Officers of Arms and are appointed by the Sovereign on the recommendation of the Duke of Norfolk in his capacity as the (rather grand sounding) Earl Marshal of England.

Above: The main hall at the College of Arms functions as the historic Court of Chivalry. Around the Earl Marshal's chair is a selection of painted wooden crests of former Knights of the Garter that once sat on top of the knights' stalls in St. George's Chapel, Windsor. The crest depicting a blue kiwi holding an ice pick belongs to the late Sir Edmund Hilary, the New Zealander who conquered Everest in 1953. The banners hanging around the wall are the personal banners of the heralds of the College.

The College has existed on a plot of land sandwiched between St. Paul's Cathedral and the River Thames since it was granted a Royal Charter by Queen Mary and her Spanish husband King Philip in 1555. The current handsome building dates from the 1670s. The main hall of the College is open to the public and often features temporary exhibitions. Since 1699 the hall has functioned as Her Majesty's High Court of Chivalry in England and Wales, a civil court in which the Earl Marshal of England, as judge, rules on the incorrect use of coats of arms.

The Court of Chivalry has not sat for centuries, save for one brief trial in 1954 at which Manchester City Council successfully argued that the Manchester Palace of Varieties theatre was displaying the city arms without authorisation. Court trials don't get much more obscure than that! Nevertheless, although the Court of Chivalry has not sat since, this curious relic continues to exist in law, and the Earl Marshal's chair occupies pride of place in the courtroom.

The College of Arms, 130 Queen Victoria Street, London, EC4V 4BT
w: www.college-of-arms.gov.uk
t: +44 (0)20 7248 2762
OPEN: Mon–Fri 10am–4pm
u: Mansion House

Guildhall
GOG & MAGOG

Guildhall is the ancient home of the Corporation of the City of London, the world's oldest continuously elected local government and the body that has governed The City for almost a thousand years. Yet the site of Guildhall has been in use for considerably longer than a millennium, as indicated by the black oval ring in the main courtyard, which marks the boundary of a two thousand year old Roman amphitheatre. The amphitheatre was one of the largest in the Roman Empire and would have been used for displays of gladiatorial combat and other gruesome forms of public entertainment.

The earliest Guildhall was probably built on or near the current location as early as the 12th century but the existing building dates to 1411 and is the City's only secular stone building to predate the Great Fire of 1666. Inside, the Great Hall is the third largest civic hall in England and has been the scene of many historic events, including the trial of Lady Jane Grey in 1553. It continues to be used for ceremonial functions and other events in the life of the City.

The hall contains many interesting features, including monuments to great heroes such as Sir Winston Churchill, Lord Nelson and the Duke of Wellington, as well as the heraldic banners of "The Great Twelve", the senior livery companies (ancient guilds) of the City of London. Most curious of all, however, are the two large statues above the Great Hall's main door. These statues represent the mythical giants Gog and Magog.

Above: The Great Hall is the third largest civic hall in England. The banners of The Great Twelve livery companies of the City of London can be seen hanging from the walls

Left: The black ring around the courtyard of Guildhall marks the boundary of London's Roman amphitheatre, one of the largest in the Roman Empire

Above: The statues of Gog and Magog continue to guard Guildhall

Various origins have been attributed to the tale of Gog and Magog, but the most popular account is that the giants were defeated in battle against Brutus of Troy, the legendary king after whom Britain is said to be named. Having defeated Gog and Magog and founded the City of London (New Troy), Brutus chained the giants to a palace on the spot now occupied by Guildhall, making them guardians of the city forevermore. And here they remain to this day.

Statues of Gog and Magog have stood at Guildhall since at least 1422 but the current wooden statues in the Great Hall date only from 1953, the previous statues on which they are based having been destroyed during the Blitz. Every year, immense wicker representations of Gog and Magog also appear in the Lord Mayor's Show, the world's oldest annual parade.

Guildhall, Guildhall Yard, London, EC2V 5AE

w: www.cityoflondon.gov.uk
t: +44 (0)20 7606 3030
OPEN: The Great Hall is open to the public when not in use. Please call for opening times.
u: Bank

Henry VIII's Wine Cellar
A REMNANT OF THE PALACE OF WHITEHALL

The Palace of Whitehall, residence of English monarchs from 1530 to 1698, was once the largest palace in Europe, its 1,500 rooms spread over 23 acres – a size unmatched even by Versailles. Originally called York Place, the palace had been the London residence of Henry VIII's close adviser Cardinal Wolsely, a vain man with a penchant for good living whose opulent lifestyle had aroused the king's jealousy. When Wolsely fell from favour in 1529 for failing to secure the annulment of Henry VIII's marriage to Catherine of Aragon, he was stripped of his assets, including York Place and the more famous Hampton Court. Henry VIII was delighted with his new properties and left his residence in Lambeth Palace to move into York Place a mere two days after taking possession, renaming it White Hall after the colour of its stone.

The Palace of Whitehall was destroyed by a devastating fire in 1698 and no major part survives save for Inigo Jones' magnificent Banqueting House, its painted ceiling a masterpiece by Sir Peter Paul Reubens that glorifies the Stuart ideal of the divine right of kings (which is rather ironic given that King Charles I passed under this ceiling to be executed on a scaffold outside in 1649).

Almost no other trace of the once great palace complex remains today except for a couple of small remnants that have been incorporated into government buildings. The most impressive of these is the large Tudor brick-vaulted undercroft that once supported the palace's great

Right: The Palace of Whitehall may have disappeared but its name lives on through a major London road that runs through the site of the old palace and which is home to many government ministries. Whitehall is now an all-encompassing term for Britain's civil service and government departments.

hall. Now known as Henry VIII's Wine Cellar, this perfectly restored chamber might have been demolished in the early part of the 20th century had it not been for an intervention by Queen Mary, the consort of King George V.

In 1938, plans to construct the current Ministry of Defence building on Whitehall would have necessitated the destruction of Henry VIII's Wine Cellar. Upon learning of this, Queen Mary obtained confirmation from Parliament that it would be saved. Rather than dismantle and reassemble the entire cellar, the engineers protected it in steel and concrete and in 1949 it was hoisted nine feet west and almost 19 feet down from its original location. It is now positioned in the basement of the Ministry of Defence, perhaps more secure than at any time in its history.

The Ministry of Defence Main Building, Whitehall, London, SW1
OPEN: Henry VIII's Wine Cellar is open by special arrangement.
U: Westminster

Above: King Henry VIII's Wine Cellar

Right: Great Hall of Methodist Central Hall – location of the first meeting of the United Nations General Assembly

Methodist Central Hall
THE INAUGURAL MEETING
OF THE UNITED NATIONS

"What is that building?" is probably the most common question asked by tourists exiting Westminster Abbey by the west doors and looking across the street. The building that excites such curiosity is Methodist Central Hall, a grand neo-baroque structure topped with a monumental dome that exudes all of the imperial confidence of the Edwardian era. Constructed between 1905 and 1911 to commemorate the centenary of the birth of John Wesley (the founder of Methodism), the hall served as the headquarters of the Methodist Church of Great Britain until 2000 and is now central London's largest conference venue.

The great hall has been the scene for many major events – including speeches by Sir Winston Churchill, Mahatma Gandhi and Charles de Gaulle – but none was more important than the inaugural session of the United Nations General Assembly in 1946, to which 51 nations sent delegations. It was at the UN meetings held at Methodist Central Hall that the Security Council and the International Court of Justice were created and the first Secretary General was appointed.

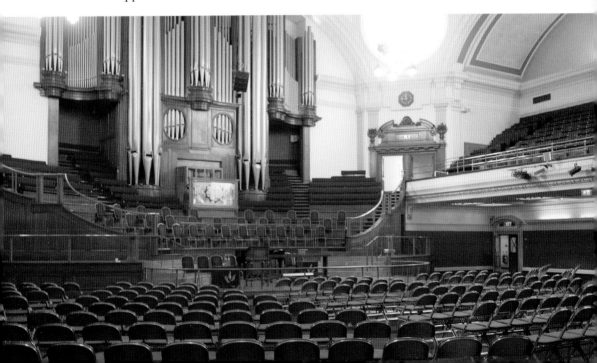

Today, beneath Europe's largest self-supporting concrete dome ceiling, the discreet use of light blue paint serves as a subtle reminder of the great hall's historic role in international affairs.

Methodist Central Hall, Storey's Gate, London, SW1H 9NH

W: www.c-h-w.com
T: +44 (0)20 7222 8010
OPEN: Mon–Fri 9am–5pm
U: Westminster

Above: Methodist Central Hall

Right: St. Olave Hart Street and the skulls that inspired Charles Dickens to dub the church "St. Ghastly Grim"

St. Olave Hart Street
"ST. GHASTLY GRIM"

A rare survivor of the Great Fire of London, the 13th century Church of St. Olave Hart Street was a thriving parish church for many centuries and is the burial place of Samuel Pepys, London's famous 17th century diarist. Buried here too are Mary Ramsay, thought by many to be the person who carried the devastating Bubonic Plague to London in 1665, and a mysterious "Mother Goose", whose name appears in the burial register for 14 September 1586. In 1554 the future Queen Elizabeth I held a thanksgiving service in St. Olave to celebrate her release from imprisonment in the Tower of London.

Left: Due to the large number of plague burials, the ground of the churchyard is raised so high that steps had to be built for people wishing to enter the church

Right: Interior of St. Olave Hart Street

St. Olave Hart Street is better known as "St. Ghastly Grim", the name given to it by Charles Dickens in *The Uncommercial Traveller*. The name was inspired by the macabre skulls that are carved on the gateway to the churchyard, and which have fascinated writers, artists and visitors ever since. The skulls, one crowned with a wreath of victory, were carved in 1658 – a sinister foreboding of events to follow. In 1665 15 per cent of London's population succumbed to the Great Plague, with over 300 plague victims buried in St. Olave's tiny churchyard that year alone. So great was the number of burials that the ground in the churchyard remains substantially higher than the surrounding area, so much so that a series of steps must be descended to enter the church.

A year later, in 1666, the Great Fire of London destroyed vast swathes of the City and lapped at St. Olave but due in large part to the effort of Sir William Penn, father of the founder of Pennsylvania, the church was saved. Penn had strong connections in the area and as an admiral and a Member of Parliament he was able to direct the men under his command to create a fire break around St. Olave and nearby All Hallows by the Tower by demolishing the buildings that surrounded them.

Having seen plague and fire visit their church in the 17th century, the skulls of "St. Ghastly Grim" saw the church gutted by bombs in the 20th century. Norway's King Haakon VII attended the rededication ceremony of the restored church in 1954 and laid a stone from Norway's Trondheim Cathedral in front of the sanctuary.

The church has strong Norwegian associations that hark back to St. Olaf (Olave) himself, an ancient king and patron saint of Norway who is said to have assisted the Anglo-Saxon King Etheldred the Unready at the Battle of London Bridge in 1014. According to legend, the

church of St. Olave is built on the site of the conflict (although historians continue to debate whether the battle ever occurred). Given this association, there was little surprise that King Haakon chose to attend church services at St. Olave whilst he and his family lived in exile in London during the Second World War.

Amongst St. Olave's more obscure historical associations is an 18th century memorial commemorating Monkhouse Davison and Abraham Newman, wealthy senior partners in Davison Newman & Co., the London grocers that supplied some of the tea chests that were thrown overboard at the Boston Tea Party of 1773, an event that helped ignite the American Revolution.

St. Olave Hart Street, 8 Hart Street, London, EC3R 7NB

w: www.sanctuaryinthecity.net
T: +44 (0)20 7488 4318
OPEN: Check with the church for opening times
U: Tower Hill

St. Stephen Walbrook
PROTOTYPE FOR THE DOME OF ST. PAUL'S CATHEDRAL

Following the Great Fire of 1666, the architect Sir Christopher Wren was assigned the formidable task of rebuilding St. Paul's Cathedral and 51 of the destroyed City churches. Such a responsibility was too great even for a man of Wren's prodigious industry and genius and so, whilst he personally completed many of these churches himself, he also engaged assistant architects to help with the design and construction of others. Of the buildings over which Wren assumed complete control, none are more important than London's parish church, St. Paul's Cathedral, and Wren's own parish church, the little-known St. Stephen Walbrook.

During his continental travels Wren had become obsessed with church domes, a feature

of French and Italian architecture that was unknown in England and which he was determined to introduce to London.

It was not by coincidence that Sir Christopher Wren started reconstruction of St. Stephen Walbrook in the same year (1672) that he started work on designs for his original plan for St. Paul's Cathedral. Wren had originally envisaged a more radical cathedral than England's conservative clergy were prepared to accept. The "Great Model" of St. Paul's which Wren constructed over 10 months between 1672–1673 remains on display in the cathedral; it comprises a building formed of a Greek cross surmounted by a giant dome, with a smaller dome above the middle of the nave. This revolutionary style would have created a vast open space in the centre of the cathedral but it was rejected by the authorities, forcing Wren to compromise and use the traditional Latin cross plan which can be seen today.

St. Stephen Walbrook provided Wren with the opportunity to experiment with his original dome design, albeit on a far smaller scale. Completed in 1679, St. Stephen Walbrook became the first domed building in England, its large central space clearly inspired by Wren's original plans for St. Paul's, and the eight arches upon which the dome rests becoming a design feature that was replicated in the later cathedral.

In a world in which domes are not unusual, the exterior of St. Stephen Walbrook is not particularly remarkable but the interior remains a stunning sight and is Wren's most perfect City church. St. Stephen Walbrook's role in the history of English architecture cannot be overstated. The great architectural historian Sir Nicholas Pevsner hailed the Grade I listed church as one of England's ten most important buildings.

St. Stephen Walbrook, 39 Walbrook, London, EC4N 8BN

w: www.ststephenwalbrook.net

T: +44 (0)20 7626 9000

OPEN: Check with the church for opening times

U: Bank

Above: The first domed building in England, St. Stephen Walbrook stands next to Mansion House and is the parish church of the Lord Mayor of London

Left: The dome of St. Stephen Walbrook

Temple Church
THE PENITENTIAL CELL

Nestled amongst the quiet alleys and courtyards of the Inns of Court, far removed from the tumult of City life, Temple Church stands in rarefied splendour, a striking relic of another age. Before the publication of the best-selling *The Da Vinci Code* in 2003, the church was one of London's best-kept secrets, seldom visited and often closed. Today, the Church is far better known and in order to cope with the increase in visitors, a small admission charge is requested from those who have not come to pray.

Temple Church was consecrated in 1185 by the Knights Templar, the great crusading order of religious knights which was formed in 1118 to protect Christians on their pilgrimages to the Holy Land. The Knights Templar took their name from Solomon's Temple, supposedly the first temple to be built on Temple Mount in Jerusalem, on the site now occupied by the Dome of the Rock.

The Knights Templar were one of the most powerful forces in Europe and Temple Church stood at the heart of their English headquarters, in the area of London today known as Temple. Now part of London's legal district, Temple originally housed the Templar residence, Temple Church, and two halls, precursors of Middle Temple and Inner Temple, the two Inns of Court that now occupy the site.

Temple Church is one of only four medieval round churches in England. The round design is based on the Church of the Holy Sepulchre in Jerusalem, the church that occupies the site on which Jesus Christ is said to have been both crucified and buried. Now part of popular culture, Temple Church has offered up most of its secrets to the public – but at least one hidden curiosity remains largely unknown.

Within the main body of the church, in the middle of the north aisle, a plain Norman door stands firmly closed to the public. Tourists pass without giving it a second glance. The keen eyed might note the narrow slit several feet above the doorway and briefly wonder what lies behind, but any interest is momentary, and they all move on. Yet this site is worthy of longer reflection, for the door leads to one of the most fiendish rooms in all of London – the Templars' penitential cell.

Located in the space above the doorway, the penitential cell was the place of

Left: The rounded arch of the Norman entrance to Temple Church predates the pointed gothic style

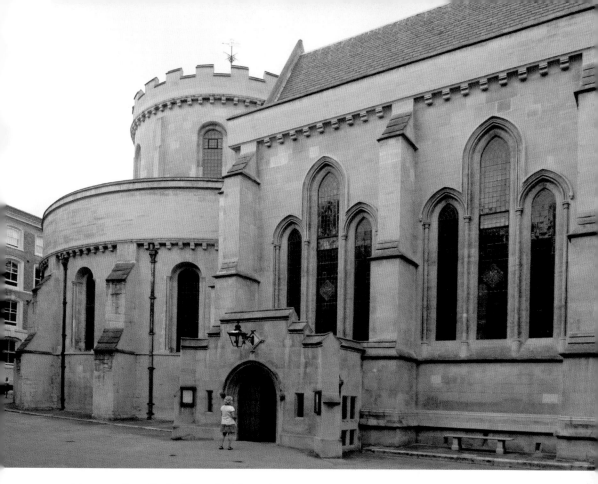

punishment for disobedient knights. Accustomed to extreme hardship on a daily basis – which often included being whipped on their bare backs by the Master of the Temple. Knights who broke the strict rules of discipline were forced to make penance by means of solitary confinement in a space designed to test their endurance.

The sadistic genius of the Temple's penitential cell is its size: it measures four feet six inches in length and two feet six inches in width, too small for any knight to comfortably stand, sit or lie. The only source of light and air is provided by two narrow slits in the wall, one of which looks toward the high altar, to enable the disobedient knight to view religious services and pray for mercy. At least one knight, Walter le Bacheler, Grand Preceptor of Ireland, died in the cell after being imprisoned for disobedience to the Master.

Above: Temple Church: One of four mediaeval round churches in England

Left: The Penitential Cell of Temple Church is located above this Norman door, its position marked by narrow slits in the walls

Above: The medieval grotesque heads around Temple Church are highly amusing

Head of the Knights Templar in England, The Master of the Temple was one of the most powerful figures in the country and was accorded an automatic seat in Parliament as the first baron of the realm. The Master's importance was such that in 1215 England's other barons agreed to meet King John at Temple to negotiate terms that would lead to the signing of the Magna Carta, one of the greatest documents in world history.

The influence of the Master and his Knights Templar could not last. Deemed too powerful by Europe's jealous kings, the Knights were disbanded in the 14th century and their wealth and property was confiscated. But more than two centuries later, the title of Master of the Temple was revived by King Henry VIII for the priest in charge of Temple Church. To this day, while his duties bear no resemblance to those of his earlier namesakes, the senior clergyman at Temple Church is known as "The Reverend and Valiant Master of The Temple".

Temple Church, Temple, London, EC4Y 7BB

w: www.templechurch.com
T: +44 (0)20 7353 8559
OPEN: Check with the church for opening times
U: Temple
ADMISSION: £

Right: Wilton's Music Hall.

Wilton's Music Hall
EAST END GLAMOUR

Wilton's describes itself as "the world's oldest surviving Grand Music Hall and London's best kept secret." Battered and shabby, this magnificent gem of British popular culture has lost none of its magic. London was once rich with music halls, the palaces of popular culture that entertained the British public with an endless variety of comic, musical and variety acts. The music halls' heyday spanned the century from 1850 to 1950, before the increasing popularity of television (very much a music hall in a box) led to their steady decline and eventual demise.

Wilton's is an odd hybrid, combining a Victorian music hall, an 18th century pub (the

Mahogany Bar) and three 18th century terraced houses. Although now famed as a precious relic of the golden age of music hall, Wilton's was not on the scene for very long. Ostentatiously decorated with chandeliers and mirrors, Wilton's Music Hall opened to great success in 1858 but had been converted into a sober Methodist Church mission by 1888. The transformation of function could not have been more extreme. For the next 70 years the Methodist mission performed sterling work for the area's considerable poor and disadvantaged. Threatened with demolition in the slum clearances of the 1960s, Wilton's was only saved from the wrecking ball by the intervention of music hall lovers including the comedians Peter Sellers and Spike Milligan and the great architectural conservationist Sir John Betjeman.

Granted Grade II* heritage listing in 1971, the building has struggled and stumbled through the decades to emerge into the 21st century somewhat the worse for wear but with a promising future. In 2007 Wilton's was entered on the World Monument Fund's "100 most endangered sites" list and it is now the focus of a fundraising campaign by the Wilton's Music Hall Trust, with the initial stage of restoration now complete.

Once again at the centre of a dynamic residential community, Wilton's hosts a variety of cultural and arts activities, often reinterpreting traditional music hall inspired performances for a modern audience. The focal point of Wilton's is the galleried concert hall with its proscenium arch. Elegant and atmospheric, the hall is a popular filming location, and played an important part in an episode of the BBC TV series *Sherlock*. The Mahogany Bar and side room have barely changed since Wilton's first opened and are now a popular gathering spot for the local trendsetters.

Wilton's Music Hall, 1 Graces Alley, London, E1 8JB
w: www.wiltons.org.uk
T: +44 (0)20 7702 2789
OPEN: Mahogany Bar: Mon–Fri 12pm –11pm; Sat 5pm–11pm
U: Tower Hill

The auditorium hall is only accessible with a ticket to an event or on one of Wilton's guided tours, available on most Mondays at 6pm.

Right: The Auditorium at Wilton's Music Hall

CHAPTER SIX

STREETS

Let me take you by the hand and lead you through the streets of London.
Show you something to make you change your mind. RALPH MCTELL – *The Streets of London*

London is a city best enjoyed by the curious meanderer. Attempts to navigate the streets urgently or purposefully can leave even seasoned travellers perplexed, defeated and intimidated. London lacks the logical grid pattern that forms the skeleton of so many great cities and few of its roads run in a straight line for very long (those that do are likely to be of Roman origin). Seen from above, the vast mass of the city is a bewilderingly complex network of narrow roads, winding streets, tiny alleys and dead ends.

Left: The Lord Mayor's Show, a parade through the streets of the City of London, is one of the world's oldest and grandest annual ceremonies

Multiple street names (London is home to 18 Victoria Roads) and an endless combination of similar sounding streets, roads, avenues, lanes, alleys, terraces, courts, places, mews, gardens, squares, circuses and crescents can frustrate even the most skilled gazeteer. The complexity of the streets explains why London's famous taxi drivers, the best trained in the world, take between two and four years to master "The Knowledge", the intensive study of the 60,000 streets or roads located within a six-mile radius of the centre of town.

And yet much of London's charm is derived from its streets. From the majestic curve of Regent Street in the West End to the jumble of medieval alleyways in the City, London's streets define the character of its districts. The human scale of London's streetscape, the proximity of the buildings and the profusion of unexpected nooks and courtyards generate a sense of intimacy that makes walking through the city an intensely interactive experience. Winding roads create a feeling of anticipation for what lies beyond every turn, and the wealth of London's historical curiosities and architectural oddities ensure that disappointment is rare.

An experienced sightseer wishing to gain a deeper understanding of the complex character of the city and its peoples would be better served avoiding the major tourist attractions (and saving the cost of admission prices!) and exploring London's rich and varied streetscapes. Dedicated enthusiasts can spend weeks, if not months, treading the pavements without repetition or boredom, delighting in distractions and relishing the risk of getting slightly lost. Devastation and development has transformed much of London, yet even the most refurbished road will contain clues and references to an interesting past. Viewing London from the outside can be the simplest and most rewarding way to discover the real city.

Street names

In the mosh pit of medieval London, with its maze of densely packed streets, it was common for trades to cluster together. The names of several streets around Cheapside, the City's ancient produce market ("cheap" was a medieval term for "market") leave no doubt of their origin: bakers baked on Bread Street, pans and other ironware were sold on Ironmonger Lane, tailors sewed on Threadneedle Street, beekeepers traded their wares on Honey Lane, cows for milking were kept on Milk Street – and no one went to Poultry looking for beef!

The streets around St. Paul's Cathedral, the spiritual heart of the City, reflect London's more pious past. Prior to the protestant reformation, members of the Catholic clergy and their acolytes recited several prayers during religious processions around the cathedral precincts, perhaps most notably during the Feast of Corpus Christi. The streets they traversed in strict sequence gradually acquired the names of the prayers with which they were associated: reciting the "Paternoster" ("Our Father") processing west on Paternoster Row, the clergy would commence the "Amen" upon reaching Amen Court. The prayers recited on nearby Ave Maria Lane and Creed Lane are similarly obvious, as is the function of Sermon Lane.

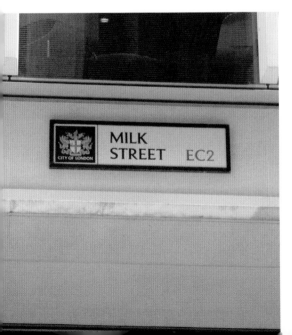

Above: The streets around St. Paul's Cathedral recall a more pious era

Below: Old signs for new: positioned above their modern replacements, these early 18th century street signs are amongst the oldest in London

Right: "Theatreland" contains the greatest concentration of theatres in London's famous West End

Right: Many major cities have a Chinatown and London is no exception

Below: Spitalfields is now home to a large Bangladeshi community but many of the street names can be traced to the arrival of French protestant Huguenot refugees in the 17th century

Trading signs

For several centuries, with street numbering unknown and much of the population illiterate, it was common practice for businesses to identify themselves by hanging symbols or illustrated signs outside their premises. Today this is most famously seen in the barbershops' striped red and white pole (a reference to the bloody bandages connected with barbers' early role as surgeons) and the pawnbrokers' three gold balls (originally the symbol of merchants in Lombardy).

In London, many historic companies have retained their unique and wholly personalised signs. Berry Bros., the world's oldest wine merchant, has traded under the "Sign of the Coffee Mill" since the 17th century, and a replica of the sign can still be seen hanging outside the St. James's Street shop. C. Hoare & Co., England's last remaining family-owned private bank, has traded under the "Sign of the Golden Bottle", ever since Richard Hoare hung a gilded leather bottle outside the Fleet Street premises in 1690. The "Sign of the Golden Bottle" remains on the bank's cheque books, debit and credit cards and hangs outside the impressive Fleet Street headquarters.

The most significant collection of trading signs reflecting this period in London's history is to be found on Lombard Street, and it is to this ancient location in the heart of the City that two of Britain's most familiar high street logos, the Barclays Bank eagle and the Lloyds Bank horse, can be traced.

Lombard Street, long renowned as the centre of British banking, takes its name from the goldsmiths of Lombardy, who received the land from King Edward I after he expelled the Jews from England in 1290. The merchants of Lombardy filled the Jews traditional roles as money lenders and much of their vocabulary remains with us today, including the terms *cash*, *creditor* and *debtor*. Even the word "bank" is said to derive from the "bancos", or benches, on which the Lombardy money lenders sat whilst carrying out their business.

Amongst the earliest known of the Lombard Street signs is the 16th century golden grasshopper erected outside the premises of Sir Thomas Gresham, founder of the Royal Exchange. The grasshopper was part of the crest on Gresham's coat of arms and a version can still be seen both on Lombard Street and above the Royal Exchange.

Right: The historic street signs of Lombard Street provide a striking contrast with the ultra-modern architecture of the ever-evolving City

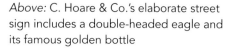

Above: C. Hoare & Co.'s elaborate street sign includes a double-headed eagle and its famous golden bottle

Above: Sir Thomas Gresham's golden grasshopper surveys London atop the Royal Exchange

Barclays Bank's association with Lombard Street dates back to 1690, however it wasn't until 1728 that the business moved to the existing "Sign of the Black Spread Eagle" (which was later numbered 54 Lombard Street). The Spread Eagle, in various forms, has remained the Barclays Bank logo ever since.

The "Sign of the Black Horse" appeared on Lombard Street as early as 1677 (at what would become number 53 Lombard Street) but it was not until a corporate takeover in 1884 that Lloyd's Bank acquired the symbol, quickly abandoning its existing beehive logo for the more prestigious Black Horse, with its Lombard Street pedigree.

Although only a handful of the Lombard Street signs survive and none are original, they remain an important historical record of London's ancient role as a centre of finance. It would be comforting to think that they serve as a sobering influence on the thousands of London bankers who pass beneath them every day; but most are probably unaware of their significance, too busy with the business of modern life to appreciate their surroundings. Perhaps it was ever thus.

Streetscapes

STAPLE INN

Described by the great architectural historian Nikolaus Pevsner as "no doubt the most impressive surviving example of timber building in London", Staple Inn provides welcome relief on this otherwise undistinguished stretch of road. Contorted and top heavy, the building is layered with character, its projecting façade pleasingly uneven. The heavily restored building, which is perhaps most famous from its appearance on pouches and tins of "Old Holborn" tobacco, dates from 1585 and affords our best impression of London's appearance before the Great Fire.

Below: High Holborn's incongruous Staple Inn

Staple Inn's name derives from its medieval function as a wool staple, a building where wool was weighed and taxed, and from its role as an Inn of Chancery, an institution originally for training clerks and students seeking careers in law. Staple Inn was once attached to nearby Gray's Inn, one of the four Inns of Court, and is the only Inn of Chancery to have escaped demolition. The Inn includes a grand hall and courtyard and provided offices and accommodation for clerks for many years before it was sold to the Prudential Assurance Company in 1886. Aside from the shops on the High Holborn side, it has been leased to the Institute of Actuaries since 1887.

Staple Inn was sympathetically restored by Alfred Waterhouse (architect of the Natural History Museum) in 1886, less sympathetically restored in 1937 and badly damaged by a German flying bomb in 1944; but, despite the passage of more than four centuries, it has managed to retain the feel of Tudor authenticity throughout.

THE "OTHER" 10 DOWNING STREET

No. 10 Downing Street is one of the world's most famous addresses, the shiny black door more recognisable than some of the British Prime Ministers who have walked through it during their residency. Until the 1980s, Downing Street was freely accessible to the public. Many Britons regarded this (and their unarmed police force) as evidence of the civility of British civic life but changing times inevitably led to the closure of the street and the erection of imposing security gates. Those who lament no longer being able to have a photograph taken outside "No. 10" are not completely out of luck, however – for whilst No. 10 Downing Street is strictly off limits, No. 10 Adam Street near the Strand makes a very good stand in. From the design of the doorframe to the colour of the brickwork, the similarity between the two houses is striking.

Above: Traffic keeps to the right outside the Strand entrance to The Savoy

Left: No. 10 Downing Street (left) No. 10 Adam Street (right)

SAVOY HOTEL ENTRANCE

One of the most frequently, and inaccurately, cited "facts" about London relates to the Strand entrance to the Savoy Hotel, which, it is claimed, is the only road in London on which cars can drive on the right hand side. While it is true that traffic must keep to the right outside the Savoy, four other London roads also reverse the UK's normal side of travel. Traffic at Hammersmith bus station, at the Gatwick Terminal at Victoria Station, on The Hale in Tottenham Hale, and at the entrance to the car park in Holly Road, Twickenham must also drive on the right. It is a shame to explode such a delightful myth, and the other exceptions are undeniably obscure and unglamorous, but so widely recounted is this story, that readers of this book who encounter it in the future will now be able to impress with this fact. And why does traffic drive on the right outside the Savoy? So that patrons using the hotel's main entrance can enter or exit a taxi from the "correct" (i.e. right hand) door.

SPLIT PERSONALITIES

When is a pub not a pub? When it is two pubs. The Ship and Shovell near Charing Cross station is a pub in two halves, tucked away on opposite sides of a cosy alley at the end of a railway arch. Both sides of the pub are attractive but the unmodernised half is particularly quirky, containing a tiny bar, an even tinier "snug" that can barely seat two, uneven wooden floors and an atmospheric panelled room upstairs known as the "crow's nest". Shovell is not a spelling mistake but is believed to refer to Admiral of the Fleet Sir Cloudesley Shovell (1650–1707), whose portrait may be seen on the pub signs.

The distinguished law bookseller Wildy & Sons Ltd. has occupied both sides of Lincoln's Inn Archway since 1830. Apart from the window displays, the scene has remained virtually unchanged for almost two centuries.

THE SCARS OF WAR

Living on an island nation that was last invaded in 1066, the citizens of London enjoyed almost nine centuries of freedom from foreign attack. That splendid isolation ended on the evening of 31 May 1915, when No. 16 Alkham Road in the London Borough of Hackney was hit by incendiary explosives from Germany's first successful Zeppelin air raid. The

Above: Wildy & Sons Ltd. has spanned Lincoln's Inn Archway since 1830

occupants and the building survived but the myth of London's inviolability had been shattered. By the start of the Second World War technological advances had brought London squarely into the enemy's crosshairs, with vast swathes of the city destroyed in the relentless bombing of the Blitz. Though most of London's bomb-damaged buildings have been demolished, restored or rebuilt, some battle scars remain – a sombre reminder of the valiant spirit of the indomitable Londoner.

During the First World War the threat of German bombing was more psychological than physical. Many Londoners feared that poison gas would engulf the city from above but in fact First World War air bombardment caused little death or destruction. Nevertheless, evidence of the Zeppelin air raids can still be found. On the night of 14 September 1917 a bomb fell by

Left: The Ship & Shovell – London's split pub

Cleopatra's Needle on the Victoria Embankment, bursting a gas main and killing a tram driver and his two passengers. The shrapnel damage to Cleopatra's Needle and the two Sphinxes that guard it remains clearly visible.

On 10 May 1941, during one of the last and heaviest raids of the Blitz, the historic Church of St. Clement Danes on the Strand was hit. Only the outer walls, tower and steeple survived the attack and the scars of the bombing can still be seen across a wide section of the outer wall at the rear. In light of its destruction at the hands of the German Luftwaffe, it is fitting that St. Clement Danes is now the Central Church of the Royal Air Force. The church holds R.A.F. services of remembrance, an annual Service of Thanksgiving, and contains many R.A.F. memorials, memorial books and gifts. Statues of Air Marshal Sir Arthur "Bomber" Harris, Bt., head of R.A.F. Bomber Command, and Air Chief Marshal Lord Dowding, head of R.A.F. Fighter Command, stand outside the main entrance to the church.

Although badly damaged by repeated hits from bombs and shrapnel, The Victoria & Albert Museum remained open throughout the Second World War ("health and safety" was not as much of a concern then as it is now!). As at many historic landmarks, volunteers provided much needed round-the-clock fire-watching protection against incendiary bombs. Two of the most powerful bombs to damage the museum exploded near its Exhibition Road entrance, badly defacing the western façade designed by Aston Webb (the architect responsible for the modern façade of Buckingham Palace). The heavily pockmarked stonework was never repaired and in 1987 an inscription was added to explain that the damage had been "left as a memorial to the enduring values of this great museum in a time of conflict."

Right: Public Shelters in Vault under Pavement: traces of London's wartime heritage are easy to find, such as this fading sign on a house in Westminster.

Above: First World War shrapnel damage to the sphinx guarding Cleopatra's Needle on the Embankment

Above: Bomb damage to the wall of St. Clement Danes is clearly visible behind the statue of Dr. Samuel Johnson

Street Furniture

gnoring the uninspired and formulaic post-war lampposts, telephone boxes and benches that blight large parts of the suburban city, London – central London in particular – is blessed with much attractive, well-designed and historically interesting street furniture. Bad street furniture can ruin a pretty view; good street furniture can enhance it dramatically.

Below: Iconic street furniture: The elegant entrance to Piccadilly Circus station enhances the famous scene

BENCHES

The Victorians were keen to improve the quality of life for city residents and are responsible for some of London's most beautiful street furniture. The wonderfully ornate benches that line the Victoria Embankment, raised on to stone dais to facilitate better views of the river, are beautiful examples of Victorian civic design and are amongst the most attractive in London.

BOLLARDS

Bollards are found across London in varying shapes and sizes but in their traditional form they usually resemble an upturned cannon – and this is because some of the oldest ones are. Unfortunately, claims that all authentic cannon bollards were captured from the French at the Battle of Trafalgar are untrue – most cannon were in fact scrap or surplus items sold by the British Government's Office of Ordnance. To add to the confusion, many later bollards were designed to look like cannon. Of the handful of authenti-

Right: Whimsical Embankment benches. Designed and installed in the 1870s, the Victoria Embankment benches were designed by George Vulliamy, the architect responsible for the pedestal and sphinxes of Cleopatra's Needle, as well as the Embankment's ornate dolphin lampposts. Vulliamy was clearly a lover of all things Egyptian as 21 of the benches near Cleopatra's Needle are decorated with winged sphinxes, whilst many of the others feature camels.

Above: A well-worn cannon bollard near the Globe Theatre

Above: Torch extinguishers flanking the entrance to a house on Mayfair's Curzon Street

cated cannon bollards that survive, the most easily accessible stand outside the Church of St. Helen's, Bishopsgate and on the South Bank of the River Thames near the Globe Theatre.

TORCH EXTINGUISHERS

In the days before street lighting, night-time journeys through London could be perilous affairs. Not only were the poorly-maintained streets full of physical hazards, but robbers could also jump out of the darkness at any moment. Linkboys were young males who, for a fee, would carry lit torches (called "links") to guide pedestrians to a sedan chair or carriage, or escort them home. Linkboys feature in the works of Charles Dickens, and were used by the diarist Samuel Pepys and the lexicographer Dr. Samuel Johnson. Many grander houses in London had link extinguishers affixed near their front doors so that linkboys could extinguish their torches after successfully taking a customer home. A few examples of these extinguishers survive intact and in situ.

Right: Each of the lampposts on The Mall is topped with a galleon, inaccurately said to represent Nelson's fleet at the Battle of Trafalgar. The statue of Captain James Cook shown here next to one of the lampposts is sculpted by the same designer.

Right: Air raid stretcher fences on a housing estate near the Oval cricket ground

FENCES

In addition to cannon, another type of war material has found itself recycled as London street furniture: air raid stretchers. During the Second World War sturdy metal air raid stretchers were mass produced to safely and swiftly transport those injured or killed during the Blitz. After the war, still fit for purpose, many of these stretchers were turned into fences. Stretcher fences are dwindling in number but a great many still survive, primarily on post-war housing estates.

LAMPPOSTS

As well-loved as any historic building, the "dolphin" lampposts that George Vulliamy designed for the Victoria Embankment are now found on both sides of the river and are

Above left: Dolphin lampposts on The Embankment
Above middle: A floral lamppost on The Blue Bridge in royal St. James's Park
Above right: Iron Lily: London's Sewer Gas Lamp

an integral part of London's streetscape. In 1870, various designs for lamps to adorn the new embankments were widely discussed in the London press. The "dolphin" lampposts, inspired by the Fountain of Neptune in Rome's Piazza del Popolo, were not the most ornate of the various proposals, but it was believed that they would look best when installed in their hundreds.

On Carting Lane behind the Savoy Hotel an elegant lamppost hides a foul secret – it is London's last sewer gas destructor lamp and the source of one of the city's most enduring myths. Nicknamed "Iron Lily", but properly called The Webb Patent Sewer Gas Lamp, the cast iron post removes unpleasant and potentially explosive gases from the sewer beneath. This peculiar function has led many tour guides and trivia lovers to mistakenly claim that the lamp is fuelled entirely by trapped methane. In truth, the gases from the sewers were never strong enough to fuel the lamp on their own but were instead drawn up the post along with the normal gas supply. The lamppost has been restored following a traffic accident and is preserved as a historical curiosity. It continues to burn 24 hours a day.

Above left: The Audley Street Lamppost: a footnote in the history of espionage
Above right: By Her Majesty's Command: The lampposts of Bow Street Police Station are colourless

"I Spy": an unexceptional lamppost on a typical Mayfair street corner holds a remarkable place in the history of Cold War espionage. Located a short walk from the US Embassy in Grosvenor Square, the lamppost on the corner of South Audley Street and Audley Square was used by KGB agents as late as the 1980s to leave discreet chalk marks indicating that a package was awaiting collection from the secret "Dead Letter Box" at the Brompton Oratory in Knightsbridge: a fact worthy of any spy novel!

Changes to policing and crime fighting tactics have resulted in the closure of many of London's police stations but until the start of the 21st century they were a reassuring presence on many London high streets, with the buildings easily identifiable from their famous blue lamps. The blue lamp has been a symbol of police stations since 1861 but Bow Street police station, the oldest and most famous in London, abandoned its blue lamps when Queen Victoria expressed her dislike of the colour during a visit to the Royal Opera House across the street. Bow Street police station closed in 1992 but the colourless lamps surmounted by crowns remain to this day.

Above: Metropolitan Police
Hook, Great Newport Street

Above: The Duke of Wellington's Horse Block
outside The Athenaeum Club

METROPOLITAN POLICE HOOK

The "policeman's hook" in Covent Garden's Great Newport Street may be London's most esoteric piece of street furniture. Relished by lovers of arcane trivia, this hook was used to hang the capes of policemen whilst they conducted traffic. The hook is unique and is believed to have been erected by a private individual in the 1930s to replace a common nail.

DUKE OF WELLINGTON'S HORSE BLOCK

Slightly to the left of the main entrance to the Athenaeum Club on Waterloo Place, two small kerbstones placed one on top of the other stand completely ignored. The passing tourist may occasionally sit on them whilst consulting a map, and a businessman or two may rest a foot on top to tie a shoelace but, otherwise, they are all but invisible to passers-by. Yet these two stones have a pedigree as distinguished as that of any club member – for they form the Duke of Wellington's horse block, erected here at The Duke's request in 1830 so that he could easily mount and dismount his horse.

GIRO, LONDON'S "NAZI" DOG

London's only Nazi memorial stands in a tiny plot of land behind iron railings in prestigious Carlton House Terrace. The memorial is a small tombstone erected to commemorate Giro, the beloved pet terrier of German Ambassador Leopold von Hoesch (1881–1936). Giro died from electrocution in 1934 after biting through a cable in the garden of the German Embassy, which was then located at 9 Carlton House Terrace. The German Ambassador was clearly upset by

this loss, as he ordered that his pet receive a proper burial on the Embassy grounds. The tombstone bears the inscription "Giro: ein treuer Begleiter!" (Giro: A Faithful Companion).

Left: Tombstone for Giro, pet dog
of German Ambassador Leopold
von Hoesch

Right: The Admiralty Arch Nose

Ambassador von Hoesch did not last much longer than his dog, dying in office in 1936. As a respected serving ambassador, von Hoesch received full state honours from the British government, including a 19 gun salute and a grand funeral cortege through London to a ship at Dover. This was the first and only Nazi funeral procession in London's history, and the image of Britain's establishment figures walking behind a coffin draped in the swastika flag as it made its way through the streets of central London is surreal.

Although dog and master received, respectively, London's only Nazi burial and only Nazi funeral procession, it would be grossly unfair to malign their reputations by associating either with National Socialism. Von Hoesch was a career diplomat who took up his office in London in 1932, a year before the Nazis came to power. The British liked him and he opposed Hitler's aggressive foreign policy. Historians have not yet unearthed any evidence of Giro's political views...

THE LONDON NOSES (A.K.A. "THE SEVEN NOSES OF SOHO")

Across central London, small prosthetic noses of various colours protrude from random buildings. For some, the London noses are as mysterious as the crop circles of the English countryside. When did they appear? How did they get there? What do they mean? Are they connected? As with any city mystery, the noses have generated urban myths. For example,

depending on the person telling the story, the nose on Admiralty Arch is said to be modelled on that of Napoleon, Lord Nelson or the Duke of Wellington and is even said to be stroked for luck by soldiers of the Household Cavalry. Another legend claims that good luck and untold wealth await those who can successfully locate each of the "Seven Noses of Soho".

Though of recent origin, the myths surrounding the London noses are now a firm part of London folklore, and there is even a "Seven Noses of Soho" guided tour. They endure despite the fact that the true origin of the noses (or at least most of them) was finally revealed in 2011. Pressured by his partner to end the mystery, the artist Rick Buckley admitted that he had erected the noses in 1997 as a subtle and silent protest against the profusion of "snooping" CCTV surveillance cameras. In an exclusive interview to the London *Evening Standard*, Buckley explained himself:

"I wanted to see if I could get away with it without being detected. The afterthought was that it would be great if these protrusions would become part of the structures themselves."

And so the mystery was solved. The noses were nothing more than plaster copies of Buckley's own nose, fixed to buildings and painted to match the surrounding walls. Buckley admitted to installing 35 noses, most of which were discovered and removed soon after their erection. Up to ten are thought to remain, most in and around Soho, including at Bateman Street, Dean Street, Denmark Street and near the Trocadero.

Searching for the London noses requires a strong neck and considerable perseverance and concentration but, as the testimonials on numerous blogs and websites attest, the exercise is rewarding. Forced to examine streets and buildings in extreme detail, the nose hunter sees London and its streets in completely new ways, discovering fine features and curiosities.

Top: The Bateman Street Nose
Middle: The Dean Street Nose
Bottom: One of these is not like the others – the splendid nose on Meard Street is probably not connected to Buckley's noses

TELEPHONE BOXES AND PILLAR BOXES

Top left: A blue police telephone post (not functional) and a traditional red telephone box add a splash of colour to this otherwise monochrome stretch of the Embankment.

Top right: London's first red telephone box. Built in 1926, this Grade II listed wooden telephone kiosk at the entrance to the Royal Academy was the prototype for the now iconic British symbol

Bottom left: London's smallest library is a disused red telephone box in the London Borough of Lewisham: the library is open 24 hours a day and users are invited to borrow, return or leave a book

Bottom right: Green telephone boxes behind the Royal Exchange

Above left: An ornate Victorian-style pillar box by the southern entrance to Tower Bridge

Above right: A pillar box on Westminster's Tothill Street painted gold in tribute to the British gold medal winners of the London 2012 Olympic Games

BROADWICK STREET WATER PUMP

Public water pumps were once a common sight in London. The long disused pump on Soho's Broadwick Street owes its survival to the important role it played in the development of public sanitation and our understanding of public health.

In the mid-19th century, London's sewer system had yet to cover the whole city, and the residents of many districts continued to use domestic cesspits for the disposal of "night soil". The contents of the cesspits were regularly dumped into the River

Right: The Broadwick Street Water Pump and John Snow Pub

Thames, at the time a source of more or less untreated public drinking water. Unsurprisingly, cholera outbreaks were common, but the means of infection remained a mystery. In the late summer of 1854, an outbreak of cholera in dirty and overcrowded Broad Street (now Broadwick Street) soon developed into one of the worst in the city's history. Over 100 people in the vicinity of Broad Street died in the first three days of the outbreak, rising to 500 a week later. Many of the residents fled.

Germs were unknown at this time but the London physician John Snow doubted the prevailing theory of the age, which held that cholera was transmitted by noxious air. Visiting Broad Street and interviewing the remaining residents, Snow quickly drew up a map in which he identified that the cholera outbreak was concentrated around the vicinity of the local water pump. The handle of the pump was removed and the outbreak subsided. Although sceptical officials replaced the handle some time later, it was eventually shown that the well had been dug a few feet away from a leaky cesspit. Snow's work is regarded as the foundation of the science of epidemiology.

The only residents of Broad Street who appeared relatively unaffected by the cholera outbreak were the monks of the local monastery. John Snow surmised that they remained infection free because

Above: In 1799 the Bank of England and the East India Company contributed to the erection of this hand pump above an ancient well on Cornhill, next to the Royal Exchange

of their penchant for beer rather than water – and so it is perhaps appropriate that John Snow is today commemorated on Broadwick Street not only by the handle-less water pump but also by the pub that stands opposite and which bears his name.

SHAKESPEARE

The Bard is London's most highly commemorated non-royal person.

The Unexpected and Overlooked

The streets of London offer the eagle-eyed explorer an impossibly rich bounty of historical trivia. Over the past 2,000 years so much has happened in a comparatively small area that it is hard to escape the presence of history. The city is cluttered with evidence of thousands of notable events but not all are obvious, and even lifelong residents can pass them daily in blissful ignorance. One of the great pleasures of walking London's streets is to divert one's attention away from the major sights in order to scour the surrounding area for historical gems, much like a beachcomber at the seaside. Many volumes can be filled with the great abundance of discreet historical signs that lie waiting for those willing to make the effort. Attempting to describe or summarise the variety is impossible in a book of this size but, by way of illustration, the following are five unexpected and overlooked historical curiosities that are within a very short walk of each other.

Below: Inscription commemorating Queen Victoria's visit to St. Paul's Cathedral to mark her Diamond Jubilee

Above: Resurgam – Divine Inspiration?

On the pavement outside the great west doors of **St. Paul's Cathedral** is a large inscription commemorating the fact that, on the occasion of the 60th anniversary of her accession as sovereign, an elderly Queen Victoria, too frail to enter the cathedral, sat in her carriage to observe the celebration of an outdoor National Service of Thanksgiving. Yet most visitors to St. Paul's are unaware of this historic event, too captivated by the magnificence of the cathedral above and in front of them to look down at their feet.

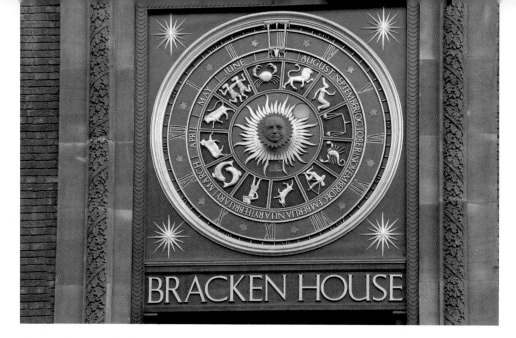

Above: An unusual tribute to wartime Prime Minister Sir Winston Churchill

Walking around the corner from the great west doors of St. Paul's Cathedral, a slightly more obscure treasure can be found on the **pediment above the south door**. Beneath a carving of a resurrected phoenix emerging triumphantly from the fire that consumed it, the word "RESURGAM" is inscribed in bold letters. Those familiar with the destruction of old St. Paul's in the Great Fire of London of 1666 will know that the architect Sir Christopher Wren almost immediately set about designing the current cathedral. As construction started and Wren attempted to set out the dimensions of the building, he instructed one of his workers to find a piece of flat stone from amongst the rubble which could be used to mark the cathedral's centre. The slab that was plucked from the ruins of old St. Paul's bore the striking Latin inscription: Resurgam ("I Shall Rise Again"). Wren took this to be a great omen for his new St. Paul's and he ensured that the word would be enshrined on the façade of the building.

Continuing along the south side of St. Paul's Cathedral to Cannon Street, the keen eyed will notice a brightly-coloured gilt metal and enamel astronomical clock on the opposite side of the road. The clock is part of **Bracken House**, formerly the headquarters of the *Financial Times*. Bracken House is named after Brendan (later Viscount) Bracken, sometime chairman of the *Financial Times* and a close friend of Sir Winston Churchill, in whose war cabinet he served as Minister of Information. In addition to the hours, the clock displays the months, the signs of the Zodiac and the phases of the moon; but the observant should hopefully also notice that the centre of the clock depicts the broad face of a stereotypically defiant Churchill. The clock is in fact a subtle tribute to Bracken's great friend and mentor.

Further along the road, diagonally across from the gleaming new Cannon Street railway station, stands a drab 1960s office block that few would be sorry to see demolished. Yet,

Above: London Stone   *Below:* Mansion House: Residence of the Lord Mayor of London

however unlikely it may seem, the instantly forgettable façade bears a precious cargo, cruelly caged behind a shabby grille. If passers-by notice the grille at all, they are likely to assume it is the covering for some form of historic ventilation shaft, yet in the aperture behind it sits "**London Stone**", the city's most ancient and mysterious talisman.

London Stone's name dates to at least 1100 (when it was known as "Londenstane") but the stone itself is possibly of Roman origin. Revered for its antiquity since the medieval era, the stone has at various times been connected to druidic worship and to Brutus of Troy, London's mythical Roman founder. The "Stone of Brutus" (as it was also known), was said to be the equivalent of Troy's "Palladium", a talisman that guaranteed the safety and survival of the city. ("So long as the Stone of Brutus is safe, so long will London flourish.")

The original function of London Stone is the subject of much debate. Some have claimed it was part of a large Roman building on the Thames, others that it was the milestone from which all distances in the province were measured, and others still that it was part of an Anglo-Saxon cross. The stone was originally far bigger than its current 43cm x 53cm x 30cm, and for several centuries it stood upright in the road, marking the centre of the city.

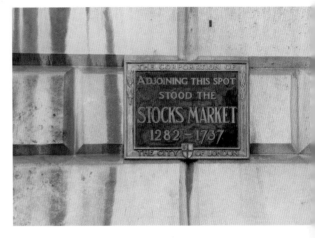

London Stone was already a well-known landmark in 1450 when the rebel leader Jack Cade struck it with his sword, declaring himself to be "Lord of London". Damaged and worn down over the centuries, the stone eventually became a traffic hazard and in 1742 it was moved to the side of the street to rest against St. Swithin's Church, into the wall of which it was incorporated in 1798. St. Swithin's was demolished in 1962 but London Stone remains in approximately the same position, lodged into the office block that was built in its place.

Passing London Stone and turning left up St. Swithin's Lane leads to Bank junction, the extremely busy intersection of several major City roads and the symbolic centre of the financial district. Faced with three of the City's most important buildings (the Bank of England, The Royal Exchange and Mansion House), the intensity of the chaotic junction was captured in a 19th century painting called "Heart of Empire". The location remains frenetic and the overwhelming sights and sounds can distract from its less obvious historical markers. For example, embedded into the main façade of Mansion House (the majestic residence of the Lord Mayor of London) is a plaque marking the site occupied by the "**Stocks Market**" from 1282 to 1737. Originally a market for selling livestock and high-quality goods, the Stocks Market developed into one of London's major trading centres. Yet, although the plaque is in plain sight, many of the high-flying stock market traders who pass Mansion House every day will be unaware of the amusing association with their profession.

CHAPTER SEVEN

RIVERS

Earth hath not anything to show more fair;
Dull would he be of soul who could pass by
A sight so touching in its majesty…

WILLIAM WORDSWORTH, *Composed upon Westminster Bridge, 1802*

The majestic view from Westminster Bridge has transformed radically since Wordsworth immortalised the magical scene he chanced upon early one morning in 1802. At the start of the 19th century the current Houses of Parliament and its famous clock tower had not been built, the South Bank was a land of wharves and docks, and the skyline was dominated by St. Paul's Cathedral, its great dome framed by the spires of Wren's City churches, jumbled together like masts in a giant flotilla.

Left: A flotilla of boats sail down The Thames as part of The Queen's Diamond Jubilee River Pageant (2012)

London may be a city of continual change but the River Thames remains its one immutable constant. The Thames is no longer a bustling waterway or the world's largest port, and it has ceased to play an important role in the daily lives of most Londoners, yet for well over 2,000 years it was London's principal artery. So all-pervading is the Thames's presence throughout the city's story, it is easy to forget that London is not a one river town. No fewer than twenty-one major tributaries cross the length and breadth of Greater London, some better known than others. The rivers of suburban London mostly flow above ground, but the many historic rivers that pass through the centre of town are now enclosed and hidden from sight, city life having transformed them into little more than open sewers.

The Fleet, the Tyburn, the Westbourne and the Walbrook are merely the most famous of the ancient waterways that were once familiar city sights and important sources of drinking water. Some were of a significant size – Elizabeth I is believed to have sailed up the river Effra to visit Sir Walter Raleigh at his home in Brixton – but most are now forgotten to history. They continue to share one characteristic, however: whilst all roads may lead to Rome, all of London's rivers flow into Old Father Thames.

Above: The Thames may look muddy but it is the cleanest metropolitan river in Europe and one of the cleanest in the world. Thanks to careful environmental and ecological management, the river which was declared biologically dead in 1957 now contains over 100 species of fish

Right: The remnants of a 6,000 year-old wooden pile from the Mesolithic era is revealed at low tide on the River Thames at Vauxhall, in the heart of London

Vauxhall
STONE AGE SPIES

Despite its prime location on the south bank of the River Thames, a short stroll from the Houses of Parliament opposite Tate Britain, Vauxhall is an area that few tourists – indeed, few Londoners – will have had reason to visit. Vauxhall's most famous landmark is the fortress-like headquarters of "MI6", Britain's Secret Intelligence Service, which squats on the riverfront next to Vauxhall Bridge. The building has featured prominently in recent films in the James Bond franchise however, for historians, this ultra-modern, high-tech building merely provides an iconic – and ironic – backdrop for a far more important structure which was discovered just metres away on the foreshore of the Thames in 2010.

There, amidst murky water, thick mud and pebbles, archaeologists discovered the remains of the oldest prehistoric bridge in Britain, an extremely rare structure from the Mesolithic period (also known as the late Middle Stone Age). London's oldest revealed structure, this 6,000 year old treasure was discovered in part because of the erosion of the foreshore by the aggressive tides caused by river flow changes resulting from new riverside construction. An unexpected benefit of otherwise regrettable environmental damage! Alas, the continued erosion now threatens the integrity of the site.

The six timber piles the archaeologists discovered are located close to the lowest tide level of the Thames, near the confluence with the tiny River Effra, one of London's ancient rivers, long vanished from public sight. The ancient bridge was constructed at a time when the Thames was much lower, and the surrounding landscape very different. Its discovery came

less than twenty years after a (comparatively recent!) Bronze Age structure from c. 1,500 BC was uncovered a few hundred metres away. Taken together, these two finds suggest that this area may have been a significant settlement for thousands of years.

The Mesolithic wooden remnants may be seen at low tide but are difficult to find (check tidal times before you travel). The nearest Underground station is Vauxhall.

Above Left: Storm channel of the River Effra next to the British Secret Intelligence Service (MI6) headquarters, seen from Vauxhall Bridge at low tide on the River Thames

Above right: Where is London's smallest cathedral? This is a trick question designed to flummox even the most knowledgeable Londoner. London's smallest cathedral is not a building but a bronze miniature replica of St. Paul's Cathedral held by Architecture, one of the eight bronze statues that decorate the piers of Vauxhall Bridge. Sculpted by Alfred Drury (1856–1944), the mini St. Paul's can only be seen from passing boats or by looking over the side of the bridge.

Right: The Thames Lions at low tide and high tide

When the Lions drink, London will sink

Lions may not be native to the British Isles but these regal animals have long symbolised Britain, its monarchy and its imperial past. The kings of the jungle have been a permanent feature in London ever since England's mediaeval kings housed them in the Royal Menagerie at the Tower of London. Today it is estimated that there are over 10,000 sculptures of lions in the British capital, the most famous of which are the four monumental bronze beasts that guard the base of Nelson's Column in Trafalgar Square. However, if legend is to be believed, there is a pride of lions that has played a far more important role in guarding the city.

Set into both sides of the Thames Embankment, gazing out onto the river, is a series of formidable looking bronze lion heads, each clenching a giant ring in its jaw. Sculpted in the 1860s by the artist Timothy Butler (who also sculpted some of the Embankment's ornamental lampstands) these lion heads most obviously functioned as mooring rings; however, according to tradition, they also served as a form of flood warning system. London policemen on duty near the Embankment were allegedly instructed to keep an eye on the lion heads to gauge the level of the river: should the water rise above the lions' mouths, London was at risk of flooding.

To ensure no one forgot the purpose of the lions, it is said that Thames Watermen created this rhyme:

> *When the lions drink, London will sink*
> *When it's up to their manes, we'll go down the drains*
> *When the water is sucked, you can be sure we're all ... in trouble*

The Thames lions may be seen on both sides of the river, but are best viewed from the riverside near Embankment Underground station.

The Westbourne
THE RIVER THAT TRAVELS BY TUBE

The Westbourne is one of the largest of London's many "lost" rivers. Starting its journey near leafy Hampstead Heath, the river flows south under Hyde Park, Knightsbridge (which takes its name from the stone bridge that once crossed the Westbourne) and Sloane Square, before emptying into the Thames by Chelsea Bridge.

Now little more than an underground sewer, the Westbourne once played an important role in London's history: for several centuries it served as a source of London's drinking water, and in the 18th century it was dammed to create The Serpentine in Hyde Park and supply water for the ornamental features in Kensington Gardens. By the 19th century, however, the clean river had become a cess pit and as West London developed in to an upper-class neighbourhood, it was gradually encased in a tunnel and hidden from sight. Yet although almost completely forgotten, the Westbourne retains a small – and unlikely – presence in London: every day, unknown to most, the river that flows under the city travels briefly "by tube" above the heads of thousands of commuters, through a large metal pipe that runs in the open air at Sloane Square station, above the platforms and across the tracks.

Sloane Square station is served by the Circle and District lines and is open during regular Underground opening times.

Trinity Buoy Wharf
LONDON'S ONLY LIGHTHOUSE AND SMALLEST MUSEUM

London is not a city associated with shipwrecks and perilous sea voyages, and so the presence of a lighthouse at the confluence of the River Thames and Bow Creek in East London's Docklands may seem incongruous. Yet London's only lighthouse shouldn't be dismissed as a curiosity – its diminutive size and odd location belie the important role it played in Britain's maritime history. As its name suggests, the Experimental Lighthouse was at the cutting edge

Left: The River Westbourne travels in a pipe above the platforms at Sloane Square station

Below: The Experimental Lighthouse and Chainstore with the O2 centre (formerly the Millennium Dome) in the background

Above: A converted lightship with the Experimental Lighthouse and Container City in the background

of new technology to help safeguard shipping – it now stands as the centrepiece for one of London's quirkiest and most innovative secret corners.

Built by the ancient Corporation of Trinity House in 1864 to stand with a neighbouring lighthouse (since demolished), the Experimental Lighthouse was a test site for maritime lighting equipment as well as a training site for lighthouse keepers. The adjoining Chain and Buoy Store, which survives to this day, served as a workshop for the great scientist Michael Faraday (famed as the discoverer of electromagnetic induction, electrolysis and benzene). As Scientific Adviser to Trinity House, Faraday spent many years carrying out lighthouse experiments in the reinforced roof space.

Since it received a charter from Henry VIII in 1514, the Corporation of Trinity House has been charged with safeguarding shipping and seafarers. Its most important modern role is as England's General Lighthouse Authority, the body responsible for the provision and maintenance of navigational aids such as lighthouses, lightships (floating lighthouses) and maritime communication systems. The Corporation established Trinity Buoy Wharf as its London workshop in 1803, principally to produce and store buoys and other water markers. Over the next 185 years, the Corporation became a major local employer, expanding the wharf to include many new workshops and engineering and testing facilities, before finally closing it in 1988.

Right: Art installation at Trinity Buoy Wharf

Above: The Faraday Effect: possibly London's smallest museum

The derelict riverside site and its heritage warehouses have now been imaginatively regenerated into a thriving hub for hundreds of people involved in London's creative communities, including artists, musicians, photographers and fashion designers. Alongside London's longest pier, home to a fleet of Thames Clippers, is "Container City", a diverse range of studios, offices, homes, workshops, eateries and exhibition and performance spaces fashioned out of recycled shipping containers.

Several notable art colleges and institutions also have a presence at Trinity Buoy Wharf, including the English National Opera, The Prince's Drawing School, Central St. Martin's School of Art and the Chelsea School of Art.

The Wharf's redevelopment has been sympathetic to its historic character and legacy, most evident in the clever conversion of two moored lightships, named LV93 and LV95, into photographic and recording studios. Michael Faraday's connection is celebrated in The Faraday Effect, an interactive installation that records the great scientist's life and times and is possibly London's smallest museum. It is open daily from 7am to 6pm.

The Experimental Lighthouse is now an art venue (open on weekends only) and is home to Longplayer, one of London's most unusual installations. Longplayer is a 1,000-year long digital composition of chimes and other ambient sounds that has been playing since the eve of the millennium, 31 December 1999, and is designed to continue, without repetition, until the end of 2999. If the ambitions of Longplayer's creator are realised, the little known Experimental Lighthouse may one day join the Tower of London as an ancient monument of the city!

Trinity Buoy Wharf, 64 Orchard Place, London, E14 0JY
w: www.trinitybuoywharf.com
t: +44 (0)20 7515 7153
OPEN: Mon–Sun. 9am–5pm
u: Canning Town
ADMISSION: Free

Right: The River Thames at Blackwall, in the shadow of the gleaming towers of Canary Wharf and directly across from The 02, the world's busiest arena – a very different scene from that which the Jamestown adventurers sailed past

Blackwall
BIRTHPLACE OF AMERICA

On a cold day in December 1606 a fleet of three ships moored at Blackwall in East London slipped into the Thames and sailed into history. On board were 105 English entrepreneurs in possession of a charter from the Virgina Company of London to establish a colony in the New World. The most famous member of their party was Captain James Smith, now immortalised through his association with Pocahontas, the daughter of a Native American tribal chief.

The transatlantic journey was grim: winter storms lashed the ships and an on-board dispute led to Smith's incarceration below deck on false charges. Landing in Virginia in 1607, these intrepid folk named their settlement Jamestown, in honour of King James I, the reigning sovereign. Jamestown was the first permanent English settlement in the New World and is considered by many to be the birthplace of America.

Above: The First Settlers' Monument at Virginia Quays

A monument to "The First Settlers", as they came to be known, was erected at their London riverside departure point in 1928. In the 20th century this part of London was not at all salubrious and the monument was vandalized and slowly fell into neglect. Thankfully, following gentrification of the area (renamed "Virginia Quays") in the 1990s, a property company renovated the site and refurbished the memorial. Now positioned directly across from the immense tent-like dome of The 02 arena, the memorial is slightly to the east of its original location. Despite its improved surroundings and its great importance to American history, the monument is barely known and rarely visited. A notable exception occurred in December 2006 when the site was briefly raised in to America's public consciousness during an Anglo-American ceremony held at the monument to mark the 400th anniversary of the ships' departure and the founding of Jamestown.

The First Settlers' Monument, Virginia Quay, Blackwall
u: East India DLR

Rotherhithe and the Pilgrim Fathers

Rotherhithe's intimate association with the River Thames is immediately evident to anyone who takes a short stroll around its cobbled streets and converted warehouses. Yet the process of gentrification that transformed this once shabby neighbourhood into an attractive district of luxury apartments and trendy restaurants makes it difficult to appreciate how vibrant and industrious Rotherhithe once was.

Rotherhithe's maritime industry peaked in the 19th and early 20th centuries, when its docks were home to a heaving mass of wharves, storehouses, taverns, barge yards, lodging houses and lightering companies. The refurbished warehouses that survive stand as imposing memorials to that energetic era. But Rotherhithe's seafaring heritage is far older – docks and shipyards have existed there since the Tudor age.

Below: Sunbeam Weekly and The Pilgrim's Pocket: A tribute to America's Pilgrim Fathers

By the early 17th century Rotherhithe was a bustling hamlet whose shipbuilders had recently acquired a royal charter from the king in recognition of their skills. It was during this period that Rotherhithe received its bit part in America's founding story. In July 1620 captain Christopher Jones, a local resident, sailed his ship from its mooring in Rotherhithe to Southampton and then to Plymouth. The ship was the *Mayflower*, a vessel destined to become one of history's most famous, its name indelibly linked with the mythology of the "Pilgrim Fathers" and their quest for religious freedom in the New World. The *Mayflower* voyage, the Pilgrim Fathers' arrival in the Americas and their celebration of the first Thanksgiving have become intrinsic elements of United States folklore.

Departing England from Plymouth, the Pilgrim Fathers named their new settlement Plymouth Colony. The colony, located in what is now Plymouth, Massachusetts, was the second English settlement in the Americas and the oldest continuously-inhabited settlement in the USA. According to tradition, the Pilgrim Fathers disembarked at a spot they named "Plymouth Rock". Had the *Mayflower* travelled to the New World directly from London, it is possible that the hallowed site might have been named Rotherhithe Rock!

Christopher Jones, the skilled Captain and Governor of the *Mayflower* voyage, left America and returned to Rotherhithe in 1621. He died a year later and is buried in the churchyard of

Above: The Flag of the USA flies from the terrace of the Mayflower pub, next to the spot from which the ship of the same name set sail in 1620

Left: St. Mary's Free School, one of the oldest in London, was founded in the 17th century by two Elizabethan seafarers to educate the sons of local sailors. In the 19th century the Watch House next door was used by watchmen to prevent bodysnatching from the adjacent churchyard

Above: The Church of St. Mary, Rotherhithe

St. Mary the Virgin, on St. Marychurch Street. Although the exact location of his burial is unknown, he is commemorated with a tablet on a wall inside the church and, outside, with a modern sculpture unveiled in 1995 to mark the 375th anniversary of the voyage. The sculpture depicts Christopher Jones, in the guise of St. Christopher, patron saint of travellers, holding a child; St. Christopher is looking back to England whilst the child looks ahead to the New World.

On American Thanksgiving Day in 2004, a descendant of the Pilgrim Fathers unveiled a local heritage blue plaque on the wall of St. Mary's Church during a ceremony attended by American and British officials. The plaque notes that Rotherhithe was home to captain Christopher Jones and was the starting point for the *Mayflower*'s epic journey to America.

Historians do not know the precise spot in Rotherhithe from which the *Mayflower* set sail, but many believe it is likely to have been next to an inn now appropriately named **The Mayflower**. This delightfully atmospheric pub is built on the site of The Shippe, an earlier alehouse that was built in around 1550. The Shippe was rebuilt as The Spread Eagle and Crown in 1780 and this in turn was renamed The Mayflower in 1957. The pub is celebrated as the only establishment in England licensed to sell American stamps!

Slightly downriver from The Mayflower, along the Thames Path, is another tribute to Rotherhithe's pilgrim past. *Sunbeam Weekly and the Pilgrim's Pocket* is an over-sized sculpture unveiled in 1991 that depicts a young boy of the 1930s reading a magazine about modern America while the spirit of the Pilgrim Fathers peers over his shoulder. Intentional or not, the Pilgrim looks distinctly surprised by the magazine's content!

**St. Mary's Church, St. Marychurch Street,
London, SE16 4JE**
w: www.stmaryrotherhithe.org

**The Mayflower Pub, Rotherhithe Street,
London, SE16 4NF**
w: www.themayflowerrotherhithe.com
u: Rotherhithe

Above right: Mayflower captain Christopher Jones as St. Christopher, patron saint of travellers

Below right: US stamps for sale at The Mayflower Pub

Her Majesty's Ships on the Thames

Three Royal Navy warships moored on the banks of the River Thames are a striking reminder of Britain's days as the world's pre-eminent maritime power. The island nation rose to global supremacy at a time when navies were the status symbol equivalent of today's nuclear weapons – and from the late 17th century until the Second World War, Britain's Royal Navy was the world's largest. Built between 1918 and 1938 HMS *President*, HMS *Wellington* and HMS *Belfast* were amongst the last vessels built during Britain's naval heyday. Long obsolete and permanently docked, the historically important ships now stand symbolic guard over London.

HMS *BELFAST*

HMS *Belfast* is Europe's largest preserved warship, the Royal Navy's last surviving cruiser and the only surviving cruiser to have been built in the 1930s. The ship was damaged by a mine in the early stages of the Second World War but, after a refit, it played a key role in the sinking of the German battlecruiser *Scharnhorst* in 1943, in the D-Day landings in 1944 and also in the Korean War from 1950–1952. *Belfast* was decommissioned in 1963 and was saved from the wrecking yard by a private trust, which opened it to the public in 1971. The Imperial War Museum has managed the ship since 1978 and it remains a popular visitor attraction.

Below: HMS *Belfast*

Right: HMS *President* painted with an artistic design inspired by First World War naval "dazzle" camouflage

HMS *Belfast*, The Queen's Walk, London, SE1 2JH

w: www.iwm.org.uk/visits/hms-belfast

t: +44 (0)20 7940 6300

OPEN: Mon–Sun 10am–4pm (4 Nov–20 Feb);
Mon–Sun 10am–6pm (21 Feb–Oct)

u: London Bridge

ADMISSION: £

HMS *PRESIDENT*

Launched in 1918 as HMS *Saxifrage*, HMS *President* is a Flower-class anti-submarine Q-ship and one of only three surviving Royal Navy warships of the First World War. Q-ships were designed to deceive German U-boat captains by resembling merchant ships, low-risk targets better sunk from the surface by conventional gun fire than by expending precious torpedoes. As a U-boat revealed itself and approached for the kill, the Q-ship would reveal its guns and counter attack the exposed vessel. Unsurprisingly, the Germans were quick to catch on to this tactic and the role of Q-ships soon changed to that of proactive U-boat hunters.

After the conclusion of the First World War HMS *Saxifrage* was renamed HMS *President* and placed in a permanent mooring on the Thames as a Royal Navy Reserve drill ship. In 1988 HMS *President* was purchased by the charity Inter-Action as a base for young entrepeneurs. Since 2006, and following a major refurbishment, she has been used as a venue for conferences and private functions and also as office space for several small companies.

HMS *President*, Victoria Embankment, London, EC4Y 0HJ

w: www.hmspresident.com

t: +44 (0)20 7583 1918

u: Temple

HMS President is closed to the public but a river bar is open on the deck on selected dates during the year. Scholars and students of naval history may visit HMS President by appointment.

HQS *WELLINGTON*

HMS *Wellington*, now known as HQS *Wellington*, is London's only floating livery hall. She was built in 1934 as one of 13 Grimsby class warships intended for service in the Commonwealth. The ship defended New Zealand's waters in the late 1930s but with the outbreak of the Second World War she was diverted to help escort convoys in the Atlantic. Over the course of the war, HMS *Wellington* saved over 450 Merchant Navy seamen and participated in the great evacuation at Dunkirk and the landings in North Africa. She was retired at the end of the war.

In the late 1940s The Honourable Company of Master Mariners, one of the famous livery companies of the City of London, was actively seeking a livery hall. For centuries livery halls have been the administrative, social and ceremonial homes for London's ancient livery companies. In 1947 due to its maritime associations, the Admiralty offered HMS *Wellington* to the Company as a floating hall. The company purchased it and brought it to the Victoria Embankment in 1938, changing its name from HMS (Her Majesty's Ship) *Wellington* to HQS (Head Quarter Ship) *Wellington*.

HQS *Wellington*, Temple Stairs, Victoria Embankment, London, WC2R 2PN
w: www.thewellingtontrust.com
T: +44 (0)20 7836 8179
U: Temple

HQS Wellington is closed to the public except on selected open days, but those with a specific interest in the sea may visit by appointment.

Below: HQS Wellington

CHAPTER EIGHT

SPACES

London is one of the world's greenest cities and boasts a higher percentage of open space than almost any metropolis of equivalent size. These facts may seem surprising. Lacking the grand avenues and public squares of well-planned cities such as Paris and Madrid, much of London can seem dense and congested. Magnificent buildings such as the Royal Courts of Justice, the Natural History Museum and the Victoria & Albert Museum would be easier to appreciate if they were situated in public squares rather than on busy roads. The contrast between the world's two finest domed churches, St. Paul's Cathedral in London and St. Peter's Basilica in the Vatican, could not be greater.

Overleaf: Most famous for Trooping the Colour (The Queen's annual birthday celebration), Horse Guards Parade was originally the Palace of Whitehall's tiltyard and was used by King Henry VIII for tournaments and jousting

Despite this, Londoners benefit from an astounding number and variety of open spaces, ranging from ancient royal parks – formerly hunting grounds of the monarch – to public commons, grand squares, historic courtyards, and tiny churchyards. Included also are the suburban parks and cemeteries designed in the 19th and 20th centuries in an effort to improve the public's physical and mental health, as well as to advance a philosophy of social engineering that used aesthetics to promote social order and a sense of personal and civic morality. All of these widely different spaces ensure that Londoners are never more than a short walk from a pleasant space in which to escape the pressures of city life.

Bunhill Fields
NON-CONFORMIST BURIAL GROUND

Bunhill Fields is London's pre-eminent non-conformist burial site, its 1.6 hectares providing a tranquil resting place for the remains of approximately 120,000 people, including some of Britain's greatest writers and radicals. The name of the site is a corruption of the slightly sinister sounding "Bone Hill", a name it acquired from its ancient use as a refuse tip for rags and bones. The name was never more accurate than in 1549 when over one thousand carts laden with human bones from the Charnel House at St. Paul's Cathedral were transferred to the field, literally creating a hill of bones covered by little more than a thin layer of soil.

Unattached to any parish church, from the 1660s onward Bunhill Fields became the preferred burial ground for radicals, non-conformists and those who did not subscribe to the established Church of England or did not wish to be buried in a religious ceremony or according to the traditional rite. In 2011 Bunhill Fields was declared a Grade I listed heritage site, a status shared by only six other London cemeteries, reflecting its national importance as the "Campo Santo" of English dissenters. With its tightly-packed assortment of 2,000 tombstones and memorials, Bunhill Fields provides a good illustration of the appearance of historic burial grounds before the Victorian development of large, landscaped cemeteries.

Many of the tombstones and memorials at Bunhill Fields have individual heritage protection, most notably those of John Bunyan, the author of the *Pilgrim's Progress*, Daniel Defoe, author of *Robinson Crusoe*, and the artist and poet William Blake, whose poem "Jerusalem" provided the words for the great hymn of the same name and which is now regarded as England's unofficial anthem.

Across from Bunhill Fields, on the other side of City Road, stands Wesley Chapel, built in 1778 by John Wesley, the founder of Methodism. John Wesley's House is also on the site and is home to the Museum of Methodism. British Prime Minister Margaret Thatcher was married in the Chapel in 1951 and John Wesley is buried in the small burial ground at the rear.

Bunhill Fields, 38 City Road, London, EC1Y 1AU
U: Moorgate; Old Street

Left: Bunhill Fields

Fountain Court &
Middle Temple Garden
THE WAR OF THE ROSES

At the heart of London's legal district, the four Inns of Court – the ancient societies to which all barristers must belong in order to be "called to the Bar" – seem to exist in a parallel reality from the heaving city that surrounds them. Ancient buildings, tranquil courtyards, green lawns and black-gowned inhabitants endow Middle Temple, Inner Temple, Gray's Inn and Lincoln's Inn with the rarefied atmosphere normally associated with the exclusive colleges of Oxford or Cambridge.

The Inns of Court each have a distinct character but they share common traits: a grand dining hall, a library, a chapel or church, courtyards and gardens. Whilst no Inn of Court claims precedence over another, 16th century Middle Temple Hall is the most historically and architecturally significant building, its treasures including England's finest double hammer beam roof and a table made from the timbers of the Golden Hinde, the galleon in which Sir Walter Raleigh circumnavigated the world between 1577 and 1580. The Hall was also host to Elizabeth I, who attended the first performance of William Shakespeare's *Twelfth Night* there in 1602.

Immediately outside Middle Temple Hall, the calm spaces of Fountain Court and Middle Temple Garden are equally distinguished. Fountain Court has an air of academic antiquity reminiscent of Eton, Harrow or one of the other great public schools. Erected in 1681, the Grade II listed fountain at the centre of the court is believed to be the oldest in London and was where John Westlock and Ruth Pinch met in Charles Dickens' novel *Martin Chuzzlewick*.

Accessible from Fountain Court via a flight of steps, Middle Temple Garden has an even greater claim to literary fame as the scene of the dispute in Shakespeare's *Henry IV, Part 1, Act 2* that resulted in the War of the Roses. Already famous for its roses in the Elizabethan era, Middle Temple Garden would have been well-known to Shakespeare and it is there that Shakespeare has rival noblemen and lawyers picking roses to demonstrate their loyalty to one of the two competing royal houses, white roses for the House of York and red roses for the

Left above: Tombstones of Daniel Defoe (left) and William Blake (right) at Bunhill Fields

Left below: Middle Temple Hall seen from Fountain Court

House of Lancaster. The rose bushes of Middle Temple Garden continue to bloom each year and in tribute to the Great Bard now also include Rosa "William Shakespeare".

Fountain Court, Temple, London, EC4Y 9DH
u: Temple

Above: The roses of Middle Temple Garden   *Right:* Friary Court at St. James's Palace

Friary Court
THE KING IS DEAD! LONG LIVE THE KING!

Inconspicuous Friary Court, an attractive but architecturally unremarkable Tudor courtyard at St. James's Palace, is possibly the most important spot in the United Kingdom. Following the death of a monarch, it is from the Proclamation Gallery balcony overlooking Friary Court that, to a fanfare of state trumpets, Garter King of Arms (the chief herald of England) first proclaims the accession of a new Sovereign. In most cities, such a hallowed location would be a celebrated attraction and a site of pilgrimage for patriots, traditionalists and history lovers. But in London, where history is frequently taken for granted, no such fuss is made – and for the thousands who pass it each day, Friary Court is nothing more than an anonymous and undistinguished annex to a little-known brick palace.

Fortunately, lovers of state ritual do not need to wait for the rare and sad event of the death of a monarch to see Friary Court ablaze with colour. Indeed, those wishing to avoid the great crowds assembled outside Buckingham Palace for the regular ceremony of the Changing of the Guard are best advised to go to Friary Court half an hour earlier (11am, or 10am Sundays) to see the departure of the Old Guard from St. James's Palace.

At 11:15am, following their inspection by the Captain of The Guard, the St. James's Palace detachment march down The Mall to join the rest of the Old Guard already assembled in the forecourt of Buckingham Palace. At the end of the ceremony, with the Old Guard returning to their barracks, the New Guard for St. James's Palace march up the Mall and place the Regimental Colour in the guardroom at Friary Court before taking up their posts.

Friary Court, St. James's Palace, Marlborough Road, London, SW1A 1BJ
u: Green Park; St. James's Park

Postman's Park

A HOME FOR HEROES

At times, big cities can seem anonymous and unfriendly, with millions of people in a seemingly endless rush, too busy to engage their fellow man, eyes fixed on phones or on the route ahead. Any person who has travelled on London's public transport can attest that the easiest way to make a Londoner squirm is to make eye contact or attempt to strike up a conversation. Yet these realities of city life do not mean that city dwellers are any less decent – humanity and compassion thrive in the urban jungle. Anyone who doubts this should visit Postman's Park, a remarkable space that tells a story powerful enough to restore even a cynic's faith in society.

Created in 1880 from the former churchyards of St. Botolph, Aldersgate and St. Leonard, Foster Lane, Postman's Park is a pretty oasis near St. Paul's Cathedral. The park's name stems from its popularity with workers from the old General Post Office Building, which stood

nearby. In 1900, at the instigation of the painter and sculptor George Frederick Watts, a Memorial to Heroic Self Sacrifice was erected in the park to commemorate Londoners who had died performing acts of selfless bravery.

The Memorial comprises a 50ft covered gallery sheltering a wall of ceramic tiles (some by Doulton) inscribed with details of 54 everyday heroes and their brave deeds. The descriptions are extremely moving and include accounts of heroes such as 17-year-old Elizabeth Boxall who died in 1888 "trying to save a child from a runaway horse" and of 12-year-old David Selves who in 1886 selflessly "supported his drowning playfellow and sank with him clasped in his arms."

A City secret for several decades, Watt's Memorial has recently re-emerged into the public consciousness, perhaps most notably through *Closer*, a 2004 film starring Julia Roberts and Jude Law in which one of the ceramic tiles is central to the story.

In 2009, approximately 80 years after the last tile had been installed, a new tile was approved by the Diocese of London to commemorate Leigh Pitt, a print technician who died in 2007 attempting to rescue a girl drowning in a canal. Further commemorations are now possible and 2013 saw the launch of "Everyday Heroes", a free mobile phone application providing details of everyone included on the memorial so far. The milk of human kindness flows thick through London.

Postman's Park, St. Martin's Le-Grand, King Edward Street, London, EC1A 4EU
u: St. Paul's

Above: Postman's Park and the Memorial to Heroic Self Sacrifice

Left: Tiles commemorating selfless acts of bravery

St. James's Square

St. James's Square, sometimes described as the grandest square in London, has been a fashionable address for over three centuries and stands at the heart of the British establishment's traditional playground. The square's elegant town houses have been home to some of society's grandest names, although today the main residents are more likely to be companies and organisations.

The centre of St. James's Square is dominated by an equestrian statue of King William III,

Below: King William III with the fatal molehill under his horse's raised rear hoof

better known as William of Orange, the protestant king who arrived in England in 1688 at the invitation of the anti-Catholic Parliament to replace James II, the Catholic Stuart king. Many of William III's supporters lived in St. James's Square and in 1697 it was proposed that "the kings statue in brasse be ordered to be set up in St. James's square, with several devices and mottoes trampling down popery, breaking the chains of bondage, slavery etc." Nothing came of this provocative anti-Catholic proposal and the king himself died in 1702, having broken his collarbone when his horse stumbled on a molehill. Opposed to the protestant monarchy, Catholic Jacobite supporters of the exiled Stuart kings dubbed the mole "the gentleman in the velvet jacket waistcoat".

The current equestrian statue of William III was erected in 1808, over a century after the king's death, and in this statue the Jacobites might be considered to have had the last laugh – for whilst the statue features none of the anti-Catholic imagery proposed for the earlier statue, it does depict the infamous molehill on which the king's horse had stumbled.

St. James's Square contains many notable buildings. Now home to the Naval and Military Club, also known as the "In and Out", No. 4 St. James's Square was once the residence of

Below: The former Libyan Embassy (left) and The Naval and Military Club, better known as the "In and Out" (right)

Above: The London Library (opposite) and Chatham House (near right)

Nancy Astor, the wealthy American socialite who became Westminster's first female Member of Parliament.

Next door to the Naval and Military Club, No. 5 St. James's Square has been the scene of tragedy. Formerly the Libyan Embassy, this building was the site of the Libyan Embassy siege of 1984 in which Police Constable Yvonne Fletcher was shot and killed. A memorial to Fletcher stands across the street from the building, on the spot where she fell.

No. 10 St. James's Square was formerly the residence of British Prime Minister William Pitt the Elder (1708–1788) and is now home to Chatham House (also known as the Royal Institute of International Affairs), one of the world's most influential think tanks. It was at a meeting here in 1927 that the famous Chatham House Rule for debates on controversial subjects was created.

The London Library has been located at No. 14 St. James's Square since 1845 and is one of the world's largest private lending libraries. The library was founded by the historian Thomas Carlyle in 1841 after his growing frustration with the policies of the British Library, such as denial of open access to the shelves. To hold the London Library's immense collection of books, the building was rebuilt in the 1890s and has been subsequently extended to enable the library to maintain its philosophy that old books should never be discarded unless they are

Right: Memorial to W.P.C. Yvonne Fletcher opposite the former Libyan Embassy

duplicates. The London Library has extremely generous loan periods and books do not need to be brought back for renewal – a book may therefore be kept in a member's house for years, with no need to return it until requested by another member.

No. 16 St. James's Square, now occupied by the East India Club, has passed through the hands of many great aristocratic families; however it was whilst owned by the socially aspiring Mr. and Mrs. Edmund Boehm in 1815 that it became the scene of its most notable historic event. On 21 June 1815 the Prince Regent (later George IV) was the guest of honour at one of Boehm's famous dinner parties. Much to the annoyance of Mrs. Boehm, a bedraggled officer interrupted dinner with an urgent message for the Prince. The officer was Major Henry Percy, the Duke of Wellington's Aide-de-Camp, and he had brought Wellington's dispatch announcing victory over the French at the Battle of Waterloo. By this time a crowd eager for news had assembled outside the building and so it was from the balcony overlooking the square that the final defeat of Napoleon was publicly proclaimed by the Prince Regent to the British public.

The 18th century Norfolk House which stood at No. 31 St. James's Square was one of London's great aristocratic town houses, a building of supreme beauty which fell victim to "progressive" redevelopers. Briefly a royal residence for Frederick Prince of Wales (the son of George II), the future George III was born here in 1738. Norfolk House remained in the possession of the Dukes of Norfolk until it was demolished in 1938 and redeveloped as an office building. Fortunately, some of the interiors were saved, and the music room may now be seen at the Victoria & Albert Museum. As commemorated by the plaques on the outside wall, during the Second World War this building was home to Supreme Headquarters Allied Expeditionary Force, and it was from here that Supreme Allied Commander General Dwight D. Eisenhower planned Operation Overlord, the D-Day Normandy Invasion of 1944.

St. James's Square, London, SW1Y 4LG
u: Green Park; Piccadilly Circus

Right: Plaque at Norfolk House, H.Q. of General Dwight D. Eisenhower for the planning of D-Day

> The United States of America recognizes the selfless service and manifold contributions of General Dwight David Eisenhower, Supreme Allied Commander, 1944-1945. At this site, General Eisenhower, on behalf of freedom loving peoples throughout the World, directed the Allied Expeditionary Forces against Fortress Europe, 6 June 1944.
>
> This plaque was dedicated by a United States Department of Defense delegation and the Eisenhower family on 4 June 1990 during the Centennial year of his birth and the 46th Anniversary of Operation OVERLORD.

Trafalgar Square

A celebration of Britain's great naval victory over France in 1805, Trafalgar Square is London's most triumphalist space. It is a square of bluster and grandeur that provides a dramatic backdrop for the many protests, rallies and parties that are held there each year. Surrounded by imposing monuments and grandiose buildings, the square's subtle charms and curiosities can be easily overlooked, but they will be found in great abundance.

At the north east corner of Trafalgar Square is a church that heavily influenced the north east corner of the United States of America. Designed by the architect James Gibbs, the restrained classical elegance of the parish Church of St. Martin-in-the-Fields became the model for many churches in colonial America and remains North America's most widely copied style of church architecture.

The plinth nearest St. Martin-in-the-Fields bears an equestrian statue of King George IV originally intended for the top of Marble Arch, which had been erected as the triumphal entrance to the courtyard of Buckingham Palace in 1828. King George IV commissioned the statue at his own expense but upon his death in 1830 it was temporarily relegated to this plinth in Trafalgar Square, where it remained forevermore. Although George IV's architectural vision made London an incalculably grander city than it was before his reign, he was so quickly forgotten by its citizens that by the end of the century the king's name had to be inscribed on the plinth.

On the south side of Trafalgar Square at Charing Cross stands another equestrian statue, this one to King Charles I. Cast in 1633 and placed there in 1675, the statue is both the oldest bronze statue and the oldest equestrian statue in London, if not Britain.

Left: More than three times life size, the statue of Admiral Lord Nelson, hero of the Battle of Trafalgar, stands atop Nelson's Column, 169 feet above Trafalgar Square

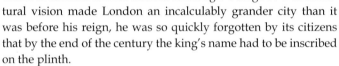

Right: The statue of King Charles I at Charing Cross marks the official centre of London. The spire of St. Martin-in-the-Fields can be seen to the right of the statue

The statue marks the official centre of London and is the spot from which all distances are measured. Prior to the erection of this statue, for more than three centuries Charing Cross had been occupied by one of the Eleanor Crosses, the elaborate markers erected by King Edward I to mark the nightly resting spots of the coffin of his queen, Eleanor of Castile, on its progression from Lincoln to London. A Victorian version of Eleanor's Cross now stands outside Charing Cross Station.

A little behind the statue of King Charles I, on the south east corner of Trafalgar Square, stands a small stone pillar topped by a lamp. The pillar is unremarkable save for the remarkable fact that it was once London's smallest police station. Hollowed out and accessible via a door on its north face, the police station was in use from 1926 to monitor demonstrations in the square and was equipped with a direct telephone connection to a nearby police station. Only large enough for one person, the pillar has not functioned as a police station for several years and is now used as a janitor's storage cupboard.

Myth buster: unfortunately the lamp on top of the pillar is not from Nelson's flagship HMS *Victory* as is sometimes claimed.

Left: Britain's smallest police station

Back on the north side of Trafalgar Square, in front of the steps that lead up to the National Gallery, a series of brass markers set into the granite pavement function as the official standards of the Imperial units of measurement (now largely superseded by the metric system). No longer need the difference between a pole, a perch, a yard, a link and a foot be in doubt! The previous standards of measurement had been kept in the Houses of Parliament but were destroyed in the fire that engulfed the buildings in 1834. To avoid a repeat of this disaster, the Standards Commission produced these markers in triplicate, installing the second set in Guildhall and the third at the Royal Observatory in Greenwich.

Trafalgar Square, London, WC2N 5DN
u: Charing Cross

Trinity Square Gardens
DON'T LOSE YOUR HEAD

Every year more than two million people visit the Tower of London to experience chilling tales of imprisonment, torture and execution. Arriving via Tower Hill underground station, visitors march in great phalanxes from tube to Tower, completely unaware that their route takes them past the site of Tower Hill scaffold, a place of execution far more dreadful than the great fortress they are visiting.

Below: Trinity Square Gardens with the former Port of London Authority building (right) and the Tower Hill Memorial (First World War (left) and Second World War (centre))

Above: Memorial to those executed on the Tower Hill scaffold

A private execution at the Tower of London was a privilege restricted to royalty and VIPs – a sort of macabre status symbol. Only a handful of official executions are recorded at the Tower of London, including three Tudor queens (Anne Boleyn, Catherine Howard and Lady Jane Grey). Nobles and commoners who had fallen from favour faced the indignity of a public execution at Tower Hill scaffold, in front of a crowd of spectators gathered in what is now known as Trinity Square Gardens.

The Tower Hill scaffold was erected in the 14th century and by the time of the final execution in 1747 more than 125 souls had journeyed there never to return. The most famous figures to die on the scaffold include William Laud, Archbishop of Canterbury during the reign of King Charles I, and Sir Thomas More and Thomas Cromwell, two great foes both of whom fell foul of the easily displeased King Henry VIII.

Given the large number of distinguished figures to have died on Tower Hill, it is surprising that the site of the scaffold is marked only by a discreet and easily missed memorial. A series of plaques surrounds a small paved area that occupies the spot on which the scaffold once stood. The central plaque bears the following inscription:

> To commemorate the tragic history and in many cases the martyrdom of those who for the sake of their faith, country or ideals staked their lives and lost. On this site more than 125 were put to death, the names of some of whom are recorded here.

Trinity Square Gardens was laid out in 1795 to form a grand setting for the headquarters of the Corporation of Trinity House, which was constructed a year later and retains its original features, including grand state rooms that are available for private hire. Granted a royal charter by Henry VIII in 1514, the Corporation of Trinity House continues to fulfil an important function as the General Lighthouse Authority for England, Wales the Channel Islands and Gibraltar.

Trinity Square Gardens was preserved as an open space by an Act of Parliament in 1797 and it contains an impressive memorial to members of the Merchant Navy who were lost at sea in the First and Second World Wars. Designed by Sir Edwin Lutyens (the great architect most famous for designing much of New Delhi), the First World War memorial on the south side of the square is a great stone corridor inscribed with 12,000 names. It was opened in 1928. The Second World War memorial in the centre of the square was opened in 1955 and takes the form of a sunken garden, its walls bearing the names of 24,000 seamen.

The square is dominated by the great white hulk of 10 Trinity Square Gardens, an imposing Grade II listed heritage building that resembles an oversized wedding cake. Originally the headquarters of the Port of London Authority, the building has been developed into a hotel and apartment complex.

On east side of Trinity Square Gardens, a small walkway on the roof of Tower Hill underground station affords a unique view that encompasses three structures built at approximately one thousand year intervals. Taken together, these structures provide the most dramatic illustration of the great sweep of London's two thousand year history. On the viewer's left, next to an 18th century statue of the Emperor Trajan, stands a piece of London Wall, the great wall that surrounded the Roman and medieval city, its base dating to c.200AD. Directly in front of the viewer stands the Tower of London's famous White Tower, built by William the Conqueror in 1078, and to the right, across the river, stands the gleaming skyscraper known as The Shard, Western Europe's tallest building and London's newest icon, completed in 2013.

Trinity Square Gardens, Tower Hill, London, EC3N 4DH

U: Tower Hill

Above: A snapshot of 2,000 years: the London landmarks that span three millennia: London's Roman Wall (left), the Tower of London (centre) and The Shard (right)

Great Britain and the United States are old allies with a shared heritage; and evidence of this closeness may be found in the large number of American memorials that can be found in London. Presidents of the United States are the largest single group of foreigners to be commemorated with London statues, most of them located by the United States embassy in Grosvenor Square. The strength of the "special relationship" can be gauged from the prominent location outside the National Gallery of a statue of George Washington, the revolutionary leader who battled Britain for American independence.

Below: The Roosevelt Memorial in Grosvenor Square was funded entirely by British public subscription in 1947 through the sale of a commemorative brochure produced by The Pilgrims, the elite society founded to advance Anglo-American friendship. The memorial commemorates Franklin Delano Roosevelt, America's longest-serving president. The

FRANKLIN DELANO
ROOSEVELT

1882–1945

UNITED STATES OF AMERICA

required funds were raised less than a week after Prime Minister Clement Attlee announced the appeal on the radio, with over 160,000 brochures sold. The statue was unveiled in Grosvenor Square on 12 April 1948 in the presence of the Royal Family, Prime Minister Attlee and Winston Churchill (who was Leader of the Opposition). The statue stands on land donated by The Duke of Westminster.

Below: The Eisenhower Statue was a gift from the people of Kansas, Dwight D. Eisenhower's home state, and was unveiled on 23 January 1989 by US Ambassador Charles Price and British Prime Minister Margaret Thatcher. The statue stands in Grosvenor Square close to the site of then General Eisenhower's base as Commander in Chief of the Allied Force (1942) and Supreme Commander, Allied Expeditionary Force (1944).

Above: The statue of President Ronald Reagan is the newest addition to Grosvenor Square and the most recent of the seven statues of American presidents in London. The statue was erected by the Ronald Reagan Foundation and incorporates a piece of the Berlin Wall near its plinth. (One of Reagan's most famous quotations is his exhortation to the leader of the USSR: "Mr. Gorbachev, tear down this wall"). The statue was unveiled on 4th July 2011 at a ceremony attended by his great friend and ally, former Prime Minister Margaret Thatcher.

Right: A piece of the Berlin Wall by the statue of Ronald Reagan

"No arsenal or no weapon in the arsenals of the world is so formidable
as the will and moral courage of free men and women"
Ronald Reagan, President of the United States, 1981-1989.
First Inaugural Address, Washington, D.C., January 20th '81.

★★★★★

RONALD REAGAN, the 40th President of the United States of America, was a privileged fighter for
freedom. With a clear vision and will, he gave hope to the oppressed and shamed the oppressor.
His contribution to world history in the 20th century culminated in his determined intervention to
end the Cold War. President Reagan has left a lasting legacy as a campaigner for global peace.

★★★★★

"With the lever of American patriotism, he lifted up the world. And so today, in Prague,
in Budapest, in Warsaw and Sofia, in Bucharest, in Kiev and in Moscow itself,
the world celebrates the life of the great liberator"
Margaret Thatcher, Prime Minister 1979-1990.

"With President Reagan, we travelled the road from confrontation to co-operation.
I join in the tribute to this remarkable man and salute him"
Mikhail Gorbachev, General Secretary of the Communist Party of the Soviet Union 1985-1991 President 1990-1991.

"I recall with deep gratitude the late President's unwavering commitment ... to
the cause of freedom as well as his abiding faith in the human and spiritual values
which ensure a future of solidarity, justice and peace in our world"
Pope John Paul II, Pontificate 1978-2005.

"We owe him our liberty. This can't be said often enough by people who
lived under oppression for half a century, until communism fell in 1989."
Lech Walesa, President of Poland 1990-1995.

★★★★★

"Mr. Gorbachev, open this gate. Mr. Gorbachev, tear down this wall."
Ronald Reagan, Brandenburg Gate speech, West Berlin, June 1987.

The Berlin Wall symbolised the Cold War in its division of East and West.

The City had been divided by Soviet troops on 13th August 1961, when overnight a barricade of barbed wire coils and
concrete posts was built along the 28.5 mile border between the Federal Republic of Germany and the German Democratic
Republic. It was later replaced by a concrete wall with watchtower patrols. Berlin was a western enclave in the middle of
the Soviet controlled East Germany, and considered crucially important to N.A.T.O.

The building of the wall was authorised by the First Secretary of the Central Committee of the Soviet Communist Party,
Nikita Khrushchev, following political tension between him and U.S. President John F. Kennedy. The instability of the Cold
War had created vast migration from the G.D.R. The wall created human tragedy for Berliners, but war was avoided and
West Berlin had been saved.

The Berlin Wall remained in place for 28 years and was finally demolished on 9th November 1989, thereby peacefully
uniting Germany and liberating Eastern Europe. The reunification of Germany and Berlin took place on 3rd October 1990.

★★★★★

In 1989 President Reagan was honoured by Her Majesty the Queen with the Knight Grand Cross of the Order of the Bath.

Above: The bust of John F. Kennedy on Great Portland Street in Marylebone was unveiled by his brother Robert Kennedy on 16 May 1965. The bust cost £50,000 and was paid for by readers of *The Sunday Telegraph*. To allow the largest number of people to donate, no donor was permitted to contribute more than £1.

Above: A bronze statue of George Washington outside the National Gallery in Trafalgar Square. Washington is depicted leaning on a fasces, a bundle of 13 sticks representing the original 13 American states. The statue is a copy of the original that stands in Virginia's capitol building and was presented to the people of Great Britain by the Commonwealth of Virginia in 1921. The statue arrived with a second gift: Virginian soil. Following the break with Britain, Washington is reputed to have declared that he would never again set foot on British soil. The statue therefore stands upon Virginian earth. A curious gift!

Above: "Allies" is a statue on Bond Street depicting Second World War allies Franklin Delano Roosevelt and Winston Churchill engaged in relaxed conversation. The statue was a gift to the City of Westminster by the Bond Street Association in 1995 to mark the 50th anniversary of the end of the Second World War. Designed to echo the Special Relationship that exists between Britain and the United States, the sculpture is interactive and people frequently have their photograph taken perched between the two statesmen.

Left: "Abraham Lincoln: The Man", also known as "Standing Lincoln", is a statue in Parliament Square that was presented to the people of Britain in 1920. The original statue stands in Chicago's Lincoln Park and was regarded as the finest American sculpture of the age.

Left: Washington D.C. is not the only city with a Lincoln Memorial. London's Lincoln Memorial was the brainchild of London pastor and anti-slavery advocate Christopher Hall and was opened in Lambeth on 4th July 1876 to serve as an international memorial to America's assassinated president. Partly funded by American citizens, the 200ft high Gothic revival tower is all that survives from a larger complex that was badly damaged during the Second World War. The tower's red and white stones are an architectural representation of the stars and stripes of the American flag.

Below: America has been associated with Grosvenor Square since John Adams, America's second president and first Ambassador to the Court of St. James, lived in a house on the corner of Brook Street and Duke Street. The house still stands and Adams' residency from 1783–1788 is commemorated with a plaque erected by the Colonial Dames of America.

The Royal College of General Practitioners

Above: As the Native American heads on its decorative façade suggest, No. 13–14 Prince's Gate has a proud American heritage. The building's first American owner was the banker Junius Spencer Morgan. Morgan purchased the property between 1857 and 1859, and on his death in 1890 it was inherited by his son, the more famous John Pierpont (J.P.) Morgan. JP Morgan lived in the house for three months every year and used it to house his impressive art collection.

In 1921 the American government accepted the offer of No.13–14 Prince's Gate as a residence for the U.S. Ambassador. The façade of the building was remodelled in the Beaux-Arts style and representations of Native American heads were placed above the ground floor windows. Eight American ambassadors lived in the house between 1929 and 1955, including former American Vice-President Charles Gate Dawes and banker Andrew Mellon. During his father's tenure as Ambassador (1938–1940) a young John F. Kennedy lived in the residence while working at the American embassy.

Above: The building was bought by the Independent Television Authority in 1955 and by The Royal College of General Practitioners in 1962. In 1980, the Iranian Embassy next door was the scene of an infamous five-day siege, with Britain's elite S.A.S. force using No.13–14 Prince's Gate as a base from which to plan its raid on the embassy. The dramatic scenes of the S.A.S. storming the embassy via its balcony (from which the flag of Iran can be seen flying in this photograph) were broadcast around the world and have become an iconic image in modern British history.

Above: Benjamin Franklin may not have been president of the United States but his status as a Founding Father and his importance to American and world history is too great not to mention his London home, which during his life also served as the de facto American embassy. Built in 1730, the Grade I listed building at 38 Craven Street is Benjamin Franklin's only surviving house and was the first site outside the USA to achieve the "Save America's Treasures" historical designation. Franklin lived in the house for 16 years and the architecturally noteworthy building retains many original features, including the floorboards, panelling, staircase and ceilings. Despite its immense historical significance, the house functioned as a hotel for much of the 20th century and it was in a dire state when the freehold was finally acquired by the Friends of Benjamin Franklin House at the end of the century. Following a sensitive restoration as a museum and educational centre, the house was opened to the public in 2006, on the 300th anniversary of Franklin's birth.

INDEXES

SUBJECT INDEX

AREA INDEX

ALPHABETICAL INDEX

PHOTO CREDITS

Except as indicated below, all photographs in this book are © Rafe Heydel-Mankoo.

Cover: Experimental Lighthouse © Trinity Buoy Wharf; Soane House (interior) by courtesy of the Trustees of the Soane House Museum © The Soane House Museum

Museums: Cover Photo © Grant Museum of Zoology UCL / Matt Clayton; Alexander Fleming Laboratory Museum © Alexander Fleming Laboratory Museum; Cinema Museum (exterior) © The Cinema Museum; Cinema Museum (interior) © The Cinema Museum; Foundling Museum (exterior) © The Foundling Museum; Foundling Museum (interior) © The Foundling Museum; Grant Museum of Zoology (exhibits) © Grant Museum of Zoology UCL / Matt Clayton; Grant Museum of Zoology (interior) © Grant Museum of Zoology UCL / Matt Clayton; Hunterian Museum (interior) © The Hunterian Museum, Royal College of Surgeons of England; Hunterian Museum (exhibit) © The Hunterian Museum, Royal College of Surgeons of England; Library of Freemasonry (exhibit) reproduced with the permission of the Library and Museum of Freemasonry © The Library and Museum of Freemasonry; Library of Freemasonry (doors) reproduced with the permission of the Library and Museum of Freemasonry © The Library and Museum of Freemasonry; The Magic Circle (interior) © The Magic Circle 2014; The Magic Circle (display cabinet) © The Magic Circle 2014; Old Operating Theatre (theatre) courtesy of The Old Operating Theatre & Herb Garret © Dazeley; Old Operating Theatre (herb table) courtesy of The Old Operating Theatre & Herb Garret © Dazeley; Old Operating Theatre (operating table) courtesy of The Old Operating Theatre & Herb Garret © Dazeley; Petrie Museum of Egyptian Archaeology (display cabinets) © The Petrie Museum of Egyptian Archaeology; Petrie Museum of Egyptian Archaeology (sarcophagus) © The Petrie Museum of Egyptian Archaeology; Royal London Hospital (interior) © The Royal London Hospital Archives & Museum; Royal London Hospital (display cabinet) © The Royal London Hospital Archives & Museum; Whitechapel Bell Foundry (exterior) © Neil Thomas for The Whitechapel Bell Foundry Ltd.; Whitechapel Bell Foundry (bell) © Neil Thomas for The Whitechapel Bell Foundry Ltd.

Shops: Berry Bros. & Rudd (exterior) © Berry Bros. & Rudd Ltd.; Berry Bros. & Rudd (interior) © Berry Bros. & Rudd Ltd.; Henry Poole & Co. (exterior) © Henry Poole & Co. Ltd.; Henry Poole & Co. (interior) © Henry Poole & Co. Ltd.; James J Fox (exterior) © JJ Fox (St. James's) Ltd.; James J Fox (mosaic) © JJ Fox (St. James's) Ltd.; James Smith & Sons (exterior) ©James Smith & Sons Ltd.; James Smith & Sons (interior) ©James Smith & Sons Ltd.;

ABOUT THE AUTHOR

Rafe Heydel-Mankoo was born in London and has lived in the city for most of his life. As a historian of the monarchy and British institutions, Rafe appears regularly on British and North American television and radio to provide expert analysis and commentary for major events and news stories.

Since the funeral of Queen Elizabeth the Queen Mother in 2002, Rafe has provided live television commentary for most of London's great ceremonial occasions, explaining the city's historical and architectural highlights to a national and international audience. Rafe holds degrees in history and law and is the co-editor of the critically-acclaimed *Burke's World Orders of Knighthood & Merit.*